DAVID BERGER

CREATIVE JAZZ COMPOSING & ARRANGING

Such Sweet Thunder

Such Sweet Thunder Publishing
www.SuchSweetThunderMusic.com

Note to the Reader

Each chapter in this book includes full and partial recordings, an in-depth anlysis, and full scores. While I would have loved to provide everything in one place, the high cost of publishing such a package would have made it impossible for me to produce, and very expensive for you to buy.

In order to make this book affordable and practical, we have put the music videos and scores online. With the scores separate from the text, you can easily go back and forth between them without having to turn pages. Each video also shows coordinated pages from the score that you can follow as you listen.

Each song has two scores, one in landscape format, and one in portrait format with a concert reduction added—all reeds and all brass parts are shown together, in concert key. Each reduction has tags showing the different techniques used.

♪ To download these recordings and scores free of charge, go to:
www.suchsweetthundermusic.com/ pages/cjca-accompanying-files

If you have trouble with the downloads, contact **information@SuchSweetThunderMusic.com**

All four arrangements in this book are featured on the CD *Hindustan* by the David Berger Jazz Orchestra on Such Sweet Thunder Records. Mp3s are available at SuchSweetThunderMusic.com, DavidBergerJazz.com, CDBaby.com, Amazon.com and all major digital music services. The personnel on the recordings are:

Conductor / Arranger: David Berger
Reeds: Jay Brandford, Todd Bashore, Dan Block, Mark Hynes, Carl Maraghi
Trumpets: Bob Millikan, Brian "Fletch" Pareschi, Irv Grossman, Seneca Black
Trombones: Wayne Goodman, Ryan Keberle, Jeff Bush
Piano: Isaac ben Ayala
Bass: Dennis Irwin
Drums: Jimmy Madison
Recorded at: Studio Berno Malmo, Malmo, Sweden
Recorded on: September 22 & 23, 2005
Producer: Roger Rhodes
Recording Engineer: Berno Paulsson
Mastered by: Peter Axelsson

Creative Jazz Composing and Arranging
Second Edition
Copyright ©2014, 2018 by Such Sweet Thunder Publishing

All the information in this book is published in good faith and for general information purposes only. David Berger and Such Sweet Thunder Publishing do not make any warranties about the completeness, reliability and accuracy of this information.

Any action you take based on the information you find herein is strictly at your own risk. David Berger and Such Sweet Thunder Publishing will not be liable for any losses and/or damages in connection with the use of this book.

If you require any more information or have any questions about this disclaimer, please feel free to contact us by email at:
information@SuchSweetThunderMusic. com.

Book and Cover Design by
Nina Schwartz/Impulse Graphics
ISBN: 978-0-692-55712-9
First Edition: October 2015

Contents

Scores / Portrait Scores with Reduction
www.suchsweetthundermusic.com/
pages/cjca-accompanying-files

> **1. Stompin' On A Riff**
>
> **2. Hindustan**
>
> **3. Do It Again**
>
> **4. The Rising Storm**

Videos
www.suchsweetthundermusic.com/
pages/cjca-accompanying-files

> **1. Stompin' On A Riff**
>
> **2. Hindustan**
>
> **3. Do It Again**
>
> **4. The Rising Storm**

Acknowledgements

Duke Ellington used to say that all through his life, people would point him in the right direction. This has been my experience as well. All my hard work wouldn't have amounted to much without the help of key people throughout my life in addition to the thousands of musicians that taught me, played my music, played music with me or sat in my classes and helped me to become a better teacher.

It's funny now that I think of it, but I don't know if I ever thanked my mother for the gift of music. Not only for my gene pool but for introducing me to classical and popular music, which started when she would play the piano at home while I was in her womb and then as a small child. My earliest memory of music is when I was two or three years old and sitting on the floor under the piano as she played. I can remember her telling me to stop messing with the pedals. I was already hooked. Those sounds coming out of our spinet were magical. I begged her to teach me how to play.

I started formal piano lessons in the first or second grade and then trumpet in 4th grade. When I was 11 and in the sixth grade, my mother thought I needed a more musically demanding piano teacher, so Mrs. Whitman taught me the classics—all of which needed to be played from memory. This skill has been invaluable throughout both my playing and conducting career. But most importantly, she taught me how to write Bach chorales. She was very strict. Voice leading was no joke. Very quickly my interest in writing music surpassed my interest in practicing the piano. One day I was playing a Beethoven sonata from memory at my lesson, and she stopped me to point out that I played a wrong pitch. I told her that I liked how it sounded, whereupon she said, "When you are playing Berger, that is for you to decide, but when you are playing Beethoven, you play Beethoven." And so I became a composer and arranger.

When I was twelve, I discovered jazz. I joined the dance band on the first day of junior high school and, within eight bars of playing the first chart, my life was decided. I had watched thousands of hours of Dinah Shore, Perry Como, Frank Sinatra, and even appearances of Louis Armstrong and Duke Ellington on TV with my mom and grandfather, but the first experience of playing swing was what did it. All of a sudden, I was catapulted into the exciting world of American popular music. I had discovered *my* music. As much as I loved classical music, it was a foreign language to me—a beautiful language, but not mine. When I played jazz, it expressed how I felt and how I saw the world. It connected me with other Americans—sophisticated adults. My classmate, Bob Schwartz, and I had no idea what we were doing, but our love for this music kept us in pursuit of how it worked.

In addition to introducing me to bebop, my first trumpet teacher, Alan Popick, assigned the melody of two songs from *Fake Book #1* every week. My mother showed me how to interpret the chord symbols, and I would sit at the piano for hours every day playing standards.

My friends and I couldn't get enough music in school, so we decided to get together after school to play our instruments. We had two alto saxes, a clarinet, trombone, piano and me on trumpet. Very quickly we realized that we didn't know what to play. The pianist pulled out a book of Gershwin piano arrangements and suggested that we play them. Since I was the only one who understood harmony and how to transpose, I was elected arranger. And so it started.

I began jazz piano lessons in 9th or 10th grade with Larry Vannata, who suggested after a few months that I write a 2-horn arrangement of *Sister Sadie*. Next up was a big band arrangement of *Well You Needn't*. When I copied out the parts and brought the arrangement into our high school dance band, I was hailed as a genius by my peers. I think it was more like a case of dancing bears—it's not how well they dance, but the fact that they can dance at all.

Our band director, Herb Schoales, was a total pro, and just about the kindest and sweetest man I've ever known. He was most encouraging and offered to help me fix up the arrangement after school the next day. We spent two or three hours going over the arrangement with him teaching me principles that I still consider to this day. I told him that I would correct everything, but he said that I had learned enough on this one, and it was time to take another tune and learn new things. Furthermore, he said that he would be happy to play anything that I wrote.

In those days most published music was pretty dreary, so I asked him if we could play some better arrangements. He asked, "Like what?" I said, "Count Basie, Duke Ellington..." To which he replied, "Duke Ellington isn't going to sell us his arrangements. If you want to play music that you like, write it yourself."

Pretty quickly I was churning out arrangements for the dance band and concert band, as well as bringing in charts to professional bands. Every spring in high school, we performed a Pop Concert. Kids would audition to sing, dance, tell jokes, and so on. The dance band sat behind them on stage in our maroon jackets and accompanied the acts. We played mostly stocks, supplemented by a

couple of specials written by our teachers. Pretty soon I was the staff arranger and was writing all kinds of vocal charts, dance charts and band numbers. At fifteen, I was in show biz and loving it.

On the weekends Mr. Schoales played bass trombone at Radio City Music Hall, which in those days was a year-round venue with first-class music and dance in addition to first-run movies. They had a big orchestra and the most superb arrangements. It was world-renown and the height of professionalism and class. Mr. Schoales brought one of my scores into the Music Hall and showed it to Ray Wright, the chief arranger. Ray told him to tell me to come up to the Eastman School of Music for the 3-week summer program that he ran, The Arrangers' Workshop.

At the same time I became enamored of Thad Jones' new big band at the Village Vanguard and asked Thad for arranging lessons. Thad introduced me to Manny Albam, who suggested that I come up to Eastman to study with Ray and him. Some coincidence!

At Eastman I was the youngest one in the program. Ray put me in the advanced class with pros, many of whom were twice my age. The focus was writing for studio orchestra. Since I had never written for strings, I suggested that I take the intermediate class, which although it was mostly comprised of adults, had some college students, who were closer to my age. Ray agreed, but also invited me to audit the advanced class. I attended both classes in the mornings, ate lunch with Manny and Ray, attended the recording sessions in the afternoons (where our arrangements were quickly and efficiently rehearsed and recorded by a professional band or orchestra with either Manny or Ray on the podium), and wrote and copied new arrangements deep into the night. The final week of the session was devoted to preparing and performing a concert, the *Arrangers'*

Holiday. That year's guests were Thad Jones, Mel Lewis, Chick Corea and Richard Davis. The first half of the concert was devoted to the students' charts. The second half featured the guest artists performing with the orchestra in arrangements by Thad, Bob Brookmeyer, Manny Albam—and me. This was the world I dreamed of being in, and here it was already.

I continued to study intermittently both privately and at Eastman with Ray for the next 15 years. Ray's analytical mind and inclusiveness prepared me for a professional career. He was the model of a true professional. He had great ears, knew all kinds of music in depth, was flexible, conducted and rehearsed at the highest level, but even more than all this, I respected him for the man he was. He treated everyone with the utmost kindness and respect. Whenever a problem arose, he was above the fray and quickly found a solution. He always seemed so secure.

When I took lessons from him, I would arrive at his house just as he and his family were finishing dinner. We'd have dessert and coffee together, and then Ray and I would repair to his studio. For the next few hours he would let me in on the deepest secrets of how music works, and then we'd hear Doris' voice from the bedroom, "Ray, the news is on," and then, "Ray, the news is over." I don't know who was sadder to end our lessons. He truly loved teaching me. I can't express how honored I felt.

One incident has stayed with me all these years and guides me in my teaching. I brought in an arrangement of *Prelude To A Kiss* that I was writing. He looked at the score and smiled. I asked him why he was smiling. He said that what I wrote was quite dissonant and dense. I asked if it was too much. He said that he wouldn't have had the courage to write it, but that it would sound good.

Starting in 1967, I spent the next four years getting my undergraduate degree in theory and composition at Ithaca College. I wrote dozens of charts for the big band at school as well as charts for professional bands, marching band, and shows. I played in pop bands and wrote the arrangements for those groups in the popular styles of the day. In school I learned classical music, not that I had any inclination to write or perform it professionally. When I heard Ravel and Debussy, they showed me how I wanted to write for strings and woodwinds. I was very intrigued by Stravinsky and also the 12-tone pioneers. At this point I started incorporating their techniques into my jazz and commercial scores.

It was during this time that Thad Jones and Paul Kondziella, independent of each other, turned me onto Duke Ellington. I had gotten so caught up in Thad, Miles, Herbie, Freddie, Horace, Trane, Joe Henderson, Chick and everything that was in style in the late '60s, that I had missed the content in Ellington's music and the beauty of that older style. I set out to learn what I had overlooked. Since no scores were available, I began to listen to the recordings and figure out the arrangements as best I could by ear. Before long I was a devoted Ellingtonian. Duke Ellington remains to this day the biggest influence on my music.

Upon graduation I returned to New York City and began my career in earnest. Within a few months I had my own rehearsal band comprised of 16 young lions, many of whom have gone on to have significant careers. We played my arrangements every Monday afternoon. I tried to write a new chart every week or two. I wanted to incorporate the personalities and talents of our musicians into the music, much in the same way Ellington did.

Shortly after Jimmy Maxwell joined our band, I began studying trumpet with him. His love of my music gave me the confidence to persevere. He not only taught me how to play the trumpet, but he welcomed me with open arms into the jazz fraternity with all his buddies—Clark Terry, Al

Cohn, Gerry Mulligan, Phil Woods, Hank Jones, et al. Beyond all this, he was a true father figure for me in my 20's. He understood me and helped me grow into a man.

In 1974 I joined the Ellington band for five months playing trumpet and doing some arranging and transcribing. Toward the end of my short stint, I started writing for a new big band that Chuck Israels put together called the National Jazz Ensemble. When I became available, I joined the NJE on trumpet. We played arrangements and transcriptions of classic jazz as well as our new compositions. Many years later, when Wynton Marsalis and I formed the Jazz at Lincoln Center Orchestra, the NJE was our prototype.

Chuck and I spent many hours discussing music, and 40 years later we are still at it. His help in organizing this book has been invaluable. I came at music from a nuts and bolts perspective. Chuck was the first person who talked to me about the aesthetics of music and jazz in particular. He gave me books to read. Years later I would learn aesthetics with Ed Green, Albert Murray and Stanley Crouch. I am deeply indebted to each of them for helping me see jazz as more than a happy collection of notes, but as the flower of our American culture and all the symbolism it brings with it. They all showed me how to verbalize what I heard and felt.

On the nuts and bolts side, my two years of study with Ludmila Ulehla not only strengthened my compositional abilities (especially counterpoint), but she showed me how to be even more critical of my own work. She analyzed every note I brought to her, and then she told me to forget all that. "You have a logical mind. Just write." There it was: write what sounds good; analyze when you get stuck.

Although my years with the NJE got me started transcribing and led to many other transcribing and arranging jobs, it was my relationship with

Wynton Marsalis and Jazz at Lincoln Center that enabled me to really learn Ellington's music. To date I have transcribed more than 500 Ellington and/or Strayhorn charts, most of which were done for JALC. In transcribing and conducting these pieces, I have come to an understanding of Ellington's aesthetic or, as Billy Strayhorn called it, "the Ellington effect." Over the past 25 years Wynton and I have spent many enlightening hours together analyzing Ellington scores. He always sees things in ways that I don't. I continue to learn from him.

When I first started writing articles, Stanley Crouch advised me to write how I speak. Chuck Israels added, "but take out the adjectives." Joan Stiles has helped me edit my thoughts into coherent writing for articles and liner notes. My deepest thanks go to Marc Schwartz, Nikola Tomic, Kelly Sargent and Nina Schwartz for their tireless work editing, organizing and designing this book. I am touched by their faith in me and my music.

Last, but not least, I want to thank all those people who have hired me to write music, conduct, play trumpet, teach and produce records. The encouragement from someone offering me a job gives me the courage and desire to continue creating music that reflects my experience in the world. That experience is informed by the era that I have lived in and the culture of my geographical location.

I had the great fortune to grow up in the richest, most diverse country in history as it was still experiencing an unprecedented confluence of fine art and popular culture. I strive to be the best me I can be, which to me means an extension of that world. My parents brought me up with icons like George Gershwin, Nat Cole and the dynamic screen personalities of Cary Grant and Clark Gable. I hope I haven't disappointed them too much. I firmly believe that if you aim high and miss, you will still hit something.

We Get Letters

Newspapers have featured advice columns for nearly 200 years, most famously *Dear Abby* and *Ann Landers* (actually twin sisters writing under pseudonyms). In that spirit I'm going to answer the most-asked questions that deal with general issues before we get to the details of arranging and composing.

1. Q: Should I become a musician?

A: No. It will make your parents very unhappy. Besides, if you have to ask, then you have already considered that you could get through life doing something else. Music, like all the arts and the priesthood, is a calling. When I was twelve, I knew. A few years later, an older musician I was working with said to me, "Being a musician is a curse, but not being a musician is a worse curse."

2. Q: Should I study classical music?

A: Yes. You may never perform any Beethoven or Mozart professionally, but the experience of playing it as a student is invaluable. As jazz performers, we need to play our instruments at the highest level. The discipline of playing classical music gives us much of the technique we need to play jazz. In order to write jazz, it is most helpful to draw on our experience playing jazz and other music. Although I haven't picked up the trumpet in over ten years, my writing is informed by what I learned playing in bands and orchestras earlier in life.

The finest classical music teaches us strong musical aesthetics. The principles are sound. I have studied harmony and counterpoint from 16th century to the present. I can't say that I have consciously used anything I learned from the early music, but the harmony and counterpoint of Baroque music formed the foundation of what I do. If you can take class-es, start as soon as possible. If not, then buy a few books on the subject and teach yourself.

3. Q: If I transcribe and study jazz soloists, arrangers and composers, will I wind up just sounding like them?

A: You'll only sound like them if you really want to. Do you sound like your parents when you speak? You learned how to talk from them, but you went on to learn from many other people and eventually you found your own voice. Sometimes I am hired to write arrangements in someone else's style. When I was young, I used to ghostwrite for a few of my heroes. It was fun to try to emulate their style. If you have more than one composer or arranger that you like, you will sound like a combination of all the things you like in their music, and ultimately discover your own musical personality that will grow out of that.

4. Q: Who are the most important jazz composers and arrangers to listen to and study, and where can I get their scores?

A: Of course everyone has personal preferences, but here are some arrangers/composers I enjoy and have learned the most from (in no particular order) Horace Silver (2-horn writing), Benny Golson (3-horn writing), Duke Ellington, Billy Strayhorn, Gil Evans, Jelly Roll Morton, Don Redman, Fletcher Henderson, Sy Oliver, Quincy Jones, J.J. Johnson,

Thad Jones, Bob Brookmeyer and Wynton Marsalis. I also love Benny Carter, Al Cohn, Neal Hefti, Johnny Mandel, Gerald Wilson, Ernie Wilkins, Billy Byers, Manny Albam and many others, all of whose work is excellent, but not as groundbreaking or influential as the first group. If I need to recommend just one, it's Duke Ellington, hands down, for the greatest depth and breadth. Jazz At Lincoln Center has published many scores by Ellington and several of the others. If you're looking for something, and can't find it, email me at **information@SuchSweetThunderMusic. com.**

5. Q: Should I write at the piano or away from it?

A: I write at the piano. So did Ellington and Stravinsky. Strayhorn wrote away from the piano and played the arrangement on the piano when it was completed. Maurice Ravel said that if you write away from the piano, you will only write what you know, but if you use the piano, you will find new things. I find this to be true for me. When I write away from the piano, I tend to write more conservatively and more from my conscious mind rather than my subconscious (which is where the best art lives). Then again, some pianists have told me the opposite.

6. Q: Do I need to write every day?

A: This is personal. I tend to write when I am inspired or when I have a deadline. I have gone months without writing a note. And then there are periods where I churn out a chart a day for weeks on end. Billy Byers said that he wrote from 9–5 Monday to Friday. I usually write during the day, but it is not uncommon for me to write late at night or very early in the morning, as my understanding neighbors will attest. Find what works best for you.

7. Q: Should I use Finale® or Sibelius?®

A: Personally, I still use pencil and paper. I grew up that way, and I am quick and efficient. I don't need to change, so I don't. I see nothing wrong with writing at the computer as long as you are making the decisions and not letting the program make them for you. Don't believe the sounds you hear in playbacks. These programs take no account of the registers and balances of the instruments. The overtones are wrong. There are sampling programs that are better, but even these can fool you. Even when I play an orchestration on the piano, I have to imagine what the real instruments will sound like. This comes from the experience of hearing music played live, playing lots of music in a variety of settings and hearing my own music played live.

After completing a score, I enter it into Sibelius® to create an engraved score and parts. I chose Sibelius over Finale® because it was easier for me to learn the program.

8. Q: What is the biggest mistake that arrangers make?

A: Overwriting. Most charts have too many notes. They are cluttered, so that the jewels get hidden. So often when I conduct the work of other arrangers, I have the horns *tacet* certain figures and lines. All of a sudden the chart becomes more focused and effective. Similarly, many charts are too long. They overstay their welcome and the audience becomes bored. It's as if the arranger were driving along the highway and missed the exit sign; the arrangement should have ended, but the arranger was having too much fun writing and forgot the big picture.

One other consideration is that the more new material in the chart, the harder it is to get a good performance from the band. This is crucial in situations with little or no rehearsal time. Sy Oliver once asked me if I wanted to know the secret to being a great arranger. He held up his forefinger (just like Curly in *City Slickers*) and said, "Just focus on one thing. Keep it simple so your audience can understand what the band is doing."

9. Q: What other arranging books should I read?

A: I started with Russell Garcia's *The Professional Arranger Composer*, which was probably the best text available 50 years ago. I haven't looked at it since, but I would imagine that the advice is still sound. It's aimed at beginners and covers the basic issues. Rayburn Wright's *Inside The Score* analyzes scores by Sammy Nestico, Thad Jones and Bob Brookmeyer. Ray was my teacher. This book is fairly advanced, and is invaluable. Bill Dobbins' *Jazz Composing and Arranging, A Linear Approach* is *the* text for small group arranging. The concepts are somewhat advanced. Lastly, Chuck Israels'

Exploring Jazz Arranging covers basic essential material and proceeds to a smattering of advanced concepts and techniques.

I studied classical composition for two years with Ludmila Ulehla. Her encyclopedic text, *Contemporary Harmony: Romantic Music Through the Twelve-Tone Row*, is the seminal book on classical harmony. The concepts presented apply to jazz as well as other Western music.

10. Q: What do I have to do to become a great arranger?

A: It sure helps to be born with talent, musicality and an artistic sense. These things cannot be taught, but if you have them, they can be nurtured. Beyond this, a great arranger needs five things: an inquisitive mind, the need to put everything in order, a good ear, boundless love of great music, and the passion, patience and fortitude to write hundreds of arrangements.

Introduction

Who is this book for?

This book is for anyone who writes, plays or listens to jazz. It explains the writing process and the construction of jazz pieces. I've attempted to answer many of the questions that arrangers and composers ask themselves when they are writing. Players who read this book will better understand the arrangements that they play and will get more from their listening, which will make them better at interpreting the music they perform. Listeners will get into the creators' heads and appreciate the jazz experience to a greater degree.

Duke Ellington's Rule

Duke Ellington had one rule when it came to music: "If it sounds good, it is good."

This has been my guiding light, my North Star. It doesn't matter to me how supposedly hip something is, how great it looks on paper, how much the musicians are sweating, how many people like it, what the critics say or how much money it makes; if I like how it sounds, it's good, and if I don't like how it sounds, it needs to be fixed or discarded. Of course, what I like may be different from what you like and different from what Duke Ellington liked. We all have personal preferences, but there are standards of excellence.

I've always figured that if I like something, lots of other people will like it as well. Popular artists need to appeal to broad public tastes (which today mostly include musical illiterates), whereas fine artists are required to trust their instincts and do what they think is good with the hope that it will find an audience. Both popular and fine artists draw upon their folk roots. Folk artists are less universal and are more frozen stylistically. They are more preservationists than creators.

Creating art involves a combination of conscious (analytical) thought and subconscious (intuitive) thought.

We listen to and analyze thousands of hours of music that get stored in our brain. When we go to create, our subconscious mixes it all up and spits out a new version. If we have never listened to or analyzed music, our subconscious will have little or nothing to draw on. The more knowledge we have stored, the more possibilities for creation. It also helps if we have some diversity in our listening and analysis.

My goal when writing is to let my subconscious do most of the work.

My conscious mind is very logical and will come up with good solutions, but they can be too linear, too simplistic. My subconscious mind is every bit as logical, but non-linear—like the difference between a story I could make up and the dream I had last night. My dream resembles my life in many ways, but on some levels doesn't seem to make sense. But when I analyze the dream, I find all kinds of symbolism and relationships that are much deeper than any superficial story I can make up.

I don't think that anyone can create music totally from their subconscious mind, unless they are asleep. Actually, I hear music in my dreams quite often. Sometimes I remember the music when I awake. I have gotten a few of my best songs this way. Not all of the music from my dreams is very good or usable. The subconscious can be as fallible as the conscious mind. We need to use our conscious mind to make choices. Possibly 90% of composing and arranging is making choices.

When I was growing up, people would always say to me that there is no accounting for taste. That never rang true to me.

I knew that Charlie Parker, Clifford Brown, Count Basie, Duke Ellington and especially Louis Armstrong were great the first time I heard them. When I was a child, after dinner on Sunday nights, my grandfather would watch *The Ed Sullivan Show*. We only had one TV in those days, so I would watch with him. My grandfather was self-educated, having left school after the sixth grade. (He had wonderful taste in clothes—I still wear his cuff links.) Although my grandmother and my mother both played piano, he knew nothing about music. But whenever Louis Armstrong appeared on Ed Sullivan's show, he would turn to me and tell me to sit down and watch the greatest musician in the world. Funny how he knew that.

Over a period of years, lesser works of art diminish in value and greater works become recognized as masterpieces. Van Gogh only sold one painting in his entire life. Fortunately, his brother recognized his genius, supported him and saved the paintings. How could the world have been so blind? Orson Welles (no less a genius) said that an artist must be out

* *Popular television variety show, 1948-1971.*

of step with his times. I would also add that greatness takes a large dose of love, hard work and faith in oneself.

It's easy to criticize others' work, but it is essential for an artist to be his own severest critic. Wynton Marsalis and I have a standing joke. Whenever I attend a premiere of a new piece of his, I go backstage and he will say to me, "What did you think? Be brutal." It takes courage to be an artist. Lots of courage.

Wynton also told me that one of the best lessons he ever got was from a non-musician/non-jazz fan who attended one of his concerts. After the show she came backstage and told him what she hadn't liked about the music. He thought about her criticism and realized that she was looking at the big picture. She could easily see the flaws that musicians and fans miss because we are too involved in the details.

The Opposites

What draws me to the arts (and to jazz especially) is that, at their best, they satisfy me both emotionally and intellectually. When immersed in them, I feel a connection to those who came before me, the universe at this moment, and even those who will come after me. Poet and philosopher Eli Siegel said,

"All beauty is the making one of opposites, and the making one of opposites is what we are going after in ourselves."

Our music must balance and integrate all the opposites: fast and slow, loud and soft, high and low, thick and thin, near and far, dissonant and consonant, long and short, rough and gentle, etc. Integrate and integrity—two words I love. They come from the Latin word integer, meaning whole. Integrate means to combine two or more elements to the point of creating a new entity. This is like what we learned in chemistry class: a mixture is putting two elements together, but a compound melds them into an utterly new thing. Integrity means having the highest moral, ethical and aesthetic character.

Motivic Development

I started writing jazz arrangements when I was 12. I had been studying the technique of writing Bach chorales for about a year. When I was 15, I wrote my first big band chart and had it played by my high school dance band. I was hooked. I wrote about 50 arrangements in high school—for the band, singers, small groups, whoever would play my music. By the time I went to college, people were hiring me to write arrangements.

One day when I was a sophomore in college I showed an arrangement of mine to a recent graduate who was a very good classical musician. We talked about it for a few minutes, and then he said something about motivic development.

I had no idea what he was talking about. I had always just written what sounded good to me. Somehow my music usually sounded pretty good. But while it was technically correct, sometimes I didn't feel as if I had hit a home run, and I couldn't understand why. And why was some music so much better than other music that seemed stylistically similar? I had thought that motivic development was just for classical music, but not jazz. Jazz is what we feel. It's our American language. What I later learned was what the movie star Jimmy Stewart said about his craft, "Don't ever let 'em catch you acting."

I've come to understand that each piece starts with a singular idea and then presents its opposite. We spend the rest of the piece proving that the opposite is really the same as the original idea. Symbolically we are exploring the oneness and two-ness of the universe. This feels wonderful to us because in the largest sense, this is what our lives are about. We exist as individuals, but are we not just a tiny bit of interconnected humanity and an infinitesimal part of existence?

Jazz Priorities
*Music is made up of rhythm, melody, harmony and tone color—**in that order.***

Any misunderstanding of this hierarchy will lead to disastrous results. How many times will an arranger be given a song with weak rhythm and bland melody, and be expected to make it work through creative harmony and orchestration? That is like trying to fix a weak play with great sets and costumes.

Most arrangers spend 90% of their time thinking about chord progressions and voicings, while giving short shrift to the rhythm and melody. Every musician studies harmony in college, but who takes courses in rhythm or melody construction?

I don't know about you, but it was the rhythm of jazz that first attracted me and still delights me. Sure, I love tritone substitution and 7-part harmony as much as the next guy, but it's still as true as when Bubber Miley first said it nearly 100 years ago, "It don't mean a thing if it ain't got that swing."

Each of these four elements of music can be further defined:

Elements of Music

1. Rhythm

Melodic (the rhythm of the melody)

Harmonic (rate and regularity of change of the chords)

Groove (the composite rhythm or the combination of all the rhythms that are happening at one time—melody, countermelody, guitar, piano, bass and drums)

Form (the macro-rhythm—the big picture).

2. Melody

The main melody

Countermelodies

Inside parts (voice leading).

3. Harmony

Chord progressions

Voicings (vertical spacings and choices of pitches)

Harmonic rhythm (rate and regularity of change of the chords).

4. Tone Color

The different sounds that can be made on an instrument

Orchestration (choice of which instruments to play certain pitches and rhythms).

Developmental Concepts

In order to tell a musical story, we need to transform the motif or motifs in a gradual way that the listener can follow the story. Certain devices have been used over and over for decades and in many cases, for centuries. The following list includes over 50 of the most commonly used in jazz. They usually occur in combination with 1, 2 or even 3 of the other techniques.

I have grouped these techniques by elements. Most often the combinations will involve one technique from each of two or more elements. For instance, the rhythm of the melody could be altered using some blue notes in a re-harmonized call-and-response pattern. This example uses one concept from each group of the four elements.

Over the past 30 years, many of my students have kept this list on their desk next to their score paper or computer, thus making it a handy crib sheet for when they get stuck.

These techniques or concepts are not the answer to any musical problems, but they can suggest paths that your subconscious can follow by filling in the details and then putting one foot in front of the other.

The object here is to use your conscious, logical mind to get your beautiful, inspired, subconscious mind back in the game. I have used short phrases (code words) to describe the transformational technique. Each is described and discussed in depth during the course of this book.

Developmental Techniques

Rhythm

Melodic
- On the beat/syncopation
- Displacement
- Repetition
- Serialization
- Lengthen/shorten phrases
- Overlap phrases

Harmonic Rhythm

Groove

Meter (4/4, 3/4, 5/8, etc.)

Style (Swing, Bossa Nova, Bebop, etc.)

Tempo

Form
- Chorus (*aaba*, blues, etc.)
- Sectional forms (march, rondo, sonata, theme and variations, etc.)
- Interlude

Melody

Diatonic

Chromatic

Blues

Serial (12-tone, 5 notes, or any other grouping of pitches that are serialized)

Register (Octave Transposition)

Octave Displacement (individual notes or groups of notes)

Repetition (entire phrases, individual notes, or groups of notes)

Sequence (Tonal or Real)

Inversion (upside down)

Retrograde (backwards)

Retrograde Inversion (upside down and backwards)

Extending Phrases

Truncating phrases (shortening)

Augmenting/Diminishing Intervals

Adding/Subtracting notes

Mixed Meter (shifting accents)

Melody, continued

Modulation
- Smooth (prepared)
- Abrupt (unprepared)
- Sequential
- Common tone
- Dominant motion

Harmony

Change of Mode (major, minor, Dorian, etc.)

Functional Chord Substitution

Non-functional (Color) Substitution

Passing Chords
- Diminished
- Chromatic (Planing)
- Dominant
- Diatonic

Re-harmonization

Pedal Point

Constant Structure

Parallel Motion

Contrary Motion

Oblique Motion

Slash Chords

Hexatonic Voicings

Symmetrical Voicings

Linearly Derived Harmonies

Orchestration

Call-and-response

Thumb Line

Pad

Solo

Unison

Thickened Line

Chorale (Spread Chords)

Tutti

Sectional

Cross-sectional

Concerto

Concerto Grosso

The Format of this Book

Art out of context is meaningless. Duke Ellington and Gil Evans used many of the same voicings and chord progressions, but their music doesn't sound remotely the same. This book provides four case studies in jazz composing and arranging, to help you move from inspiration to orchestration to performance. Buying this book gives you access to four scores that I wrote, linked to my band's performances of them. For each one, I walk you through how I wanted to tell the musical story, how I went about it, what worked, what didn't work, and how it came out. I'm sharing tools that should allow you to conceive and write arrangements that showcase your own conception—not Ellington's, nor Gil's, nor mine.

While most arranging and composition books are set up to present a logical progression of concepts and techniques with short, written musical examples, I have chosen a different route. I explain concepts and techniques within the context of full big band arrangements that you can listen to. Understanding the context may be as important as understanding the concepts and techniques. Seeing how these things live in their surroundings gives us a much better idea of what constitutes good artistic choices.

Each chapter in this book includes full and partial **music videos**, an **in-depth analysis**, and two versions of the **full score**.

The first is the original score, in landscape format. (You'll see this score as you listen to the music videos.) The second is the same score in portrait format with a concert reduction—reeds and brass parts are also shown in four staves at the bottom of each page, in concert key. No transposition is necessary.

All the tracks are well-played and well-recorded, so you don't have to imagine what they might sound like. The four tracks I have chosen are from my CD *Hindustan* on Such Sweet Thunder (SST1004). These four arrangements represent varied styles and present many different rhythmic, melodic, harmonic and orchestration situations. Mostly, I'm interested in how each piece unfolds—its development.

Getting Started

Find the videos and scores at:
www.suchsweetthundermusic.com/ pages/cjca-accompanying-files

(If you have trouble downloading, contact: information@suchsweetthundermusic.com.)

Let's get to work.

Analyses

1. Stompin' On A Riff

[At www.suchsweetthundermusic.com/pages/cjca-accompanying-files listen to **1-1: Complete Arrangement**. Now ask yourself these three questions that I ask myself whenever I listen to music:

1. What do you like about this chart?
2. What don't you like?
3. How might you do it differently?]

The Opening Number

I originally wrote this chart with the idea of having it published and played by high school jazz bands. At the same time I wanted to write something I could play with my band. I was thinking of something in the Basie style—simple and straight-ahead, but most of all swinging—something that would make a good opening number—to the point, and not too long.

The Central Motif

Stompin' On A Riff is based on a 3-note upwardly chromatic riff *(sol, si, la)*—half rest, quarter and two 8th notes, the second 8th being tied over to a whole note.

Example 1-1

Aside from the emphasis on the 6th, which connotes wonder and happiness, this motif in itself is nothing spectacular. Melodically it is the same motif at the heart of *Mack The Knife* and a pile of other songs. What makes this chart different from all the rest is the development.

Development

Development is what separates the competent arranger/composer from the best, or as we used to say, the men from the boys. (If you know Mary Lou Williams' music at all, you'd know that this cliché does not and never did apply to jazz).

Creating Your Own Style

I wasn't consciously trying to copy any arranger's style, but it turned out to reflect the work of two of my heroes, Benny Carter (listen to *Miss Missouri* and *Vine Street Rumble* from **Kansas City Suite**) and Neal Hefti *(Splanky* from **The Atomic Mr. Basie).** Count Basie recorded both records in 1958. If you listen to these sides (and I strongly suggest that you listen to lots of their music, because they are two of the best and most influential jazz arrangers —they valued simplicity above all else, making their music a great place to start) you will notice that although we share a concentration on riffs, call-and-response, lots of unison, 4-part close harmonies, sectional writing, swinging rhythms and conciseness, I have created my own take on the Basie style. I didn't set out to be different, but my personal taste just led me there.

A Few Personal Confessions

1. I had to rewrite this chart a few times until I got it right. No shame in that. Beethoven did it. At times even Ellington and Strayhorn did it. I have my own big band, and if something doesn't feel quite right, I have the luxury to dictate changes on the spot in rehearsal or take the score home and perform more invasive surgery. I wanted this chart to be simple, but not simplistic. Although it is not difficult to play, I want the band and the audience to (as my mentor Jimmy Maxwell used to say) "wiggle their asses, stomp their feet and holler." At no time do I ever want to apologize and say that this chart was written for students. When I write for students, I limit the technical problems, but still expect them to deal with sophisticated musical issues (especially, but not limited to swinging and blues inflection).

2. I wrote the intro after the entire first draft of this chart was written. Rewriting intros is not uncommon for me. Most times I start writing at letter **A**, and when I know the intro, I go back and write it. I've found that if I write the intro first I usually wind up throwing it out or rewriting it, because before I write the chart, I don't know what it is that I am introducing. Also there have been times where I have written arrangements out of order, or removed pages. Ellington was notorious for this type of behavior.

3. 95% of what I will be talking about in these analyses was unknown to me on a conscious level while I was writing these arrangements. It was only when I sat down to write this book that I figured out what I had done, and why it makes sense. The 95% came from my subconscious mind. All the years of listening, playing and studying music have gotten stored somewhere in my brain. When I write music, I tap into that part of my subconscious mind where everything gets mixed up together, and I weave a story from the sounds I can retrieve and piece them together in ways that satisfy my need to bring order out of chaos and find meaning in my life. Without all the listening, playing and study, I would have little to draw on.

4. Sometimes what I write doesn't seem quite right to me. It may be extraneous, out of character, trite, too simplistic, etc. When this happens, I step back, analyze the situation and use my conscious brain to tidy things up. Or sometimes I'm just stuck. I can't figure out where to go. Again, I step back, analyze the situation, and see if I can consciously come up with a direction. I use knowledge gained from listening to and analyzing scores that I admire as well as my experience creating my own works. It's amazing, but it doesn't take but a minute or two before my subconscious mind kicks in, and I'm in that happy place again.

5. It's not that my conscious mind goes to sleep while the subconscious is creating. It's like all that knowledge is in the back of my head chattering away. Sometimes the suggestions it makes are useful, and then the subconscious will pluck them up and run with them. A lot of the time the conscious mind is occupied with the mechanics of writing music: notation, penmanship, sharpening pencils, etc., while the subconscious is spilling out music faster than I can get it on the paper. When I was young, it was a challenge to remember what I had thought of a few minutes ago. Years of practice have made me better at handling this.

Form

I was once involved in a documentary on Neil Simon, where he spoke about how he started out as a TV comedy writer for Sid Caesar. After a few years, he told the other writers that he wanted to write plays. They hipped him to a well-known and respected book on playwriting. In the book the author talked about form and the need to plan out the entire plot before filling in the details. Doc said that he tried to do that, but when he started the actual writing, the characters wanted to say and do other things. I had exactly the same experience when I first started arranging and composing. I found that any time I try to force my logic

STOMPIN' ON A RIFF

onto a situation, it never feels organic. Sometimes I'll be writing a chart, and I'll think of a great ending. Nine times out of ten, when I get to the ending, the one I had planned doesn't seem appropriate.

All this said, form is the make or break of an arrangement or composition.

The form determines if we are interested and ultimately, if we feel satisfied. Understanding form in music, all the arts, life, nature and the universe helps us to balance and shape our work. I'm a pretty analytical guy. When I listen to music, one part of me is just feeling, and the other part of me is recognizing the structure and techniques at work. Great art must satisfy both. Most musicians have an innate sense of form. I recommend dissecting the music you play and listen to, but never substituting logic for what feels good. Let them complement each other. The form of **Stompin' On A Riff** (keys are in parentheses):

> Intro (G) 8 bars
> Piano solo—1 chorus (32 bars—abab)
> Head—1 chorus
> Trumpet solo—1 chorus (A♭)
> Alto Sax solo—1 chorus
> Shout Chorus—½ chorus soft (E♭),
> ½ chorus loud (B♭)
> Recap—32 bars—the **A** section played
> 4 times (G)
> Coda—6 bars

[Listen again to **1-1: Complete Arrangement** with the form in mind. See how each section is at once surprising and inevitable. The seams are covered up, so that the entire piece feels of one cloth. There is an arc to the form, which gives us a feeling of satisfaction at the end. The musicians (and good dancers and even some good listeners) feel the form intuitively. It's like driving down the highway and knowing that your exit is coming

up because it just feels like enough time has elapsed. An arranger must be keenly aware of not only what to do, but when to do it. While you are listening, see if you think the proportions are right.]

The Intro

For me, the intro is the hardest part of the arrangement to write. I have been known to rewrite intros several times until I get them right.

*A good intro should not only set the mood and tempo (in the great majority of cases), but it should allude to the main motif of the piece (possibly in an obscure way), so that when the theme occurs at letter **A**, it feels like we are already familiar with it.*

In some cases the groove is set up in the intro and the motif is established at Letter **A**. Conversely there are times when the motif is stated in the intro, and the groove first appears at letter **A**. The latter is the case in **Stompin' On A Riff**.

The intro is the promise, and whatever is promised had better be fulfilled later on, or everyone (listeners, performers and arranger) will feel cheated.

On rare occasions I complete an entire chart and still don't know what the intro is. Sometimes the best solution is no intro at all. This frequently happens with tunes that start with a break, a stop-time, or even a pick-up.

Using the Motif in the Intro

In **Stompin' On A Riff** the piano starts by itself—typical Count Basie. The right hand is triadic half notes with inverted tonic pedal point (repeated G's on top) while the harmonies move: G/B B♭° Am7 A#°. This is the retrograde (backwards) of the Basie piano signature Am7 A#° G/B. The left hand counters with dominant pedal point (repeated D's) on beats 2 and 4. This happens three times, which sets up the idea of a riff-oriented piece (in case you missed the title). In the standard Basie intro set-up, bars **7–8** contain a chromatic melody going from the 3rd to the 5th leading up to a dominant 7th with an augmented 5th.

So, what seems to be a generic Basie intro turns out to be totally derived from the motif at **A**. Instead of D, D#, E, we start with the inversion (upside down) in 3rds transposed down a step (D, D♭, C) and down a 4th (B, B♭, A), then invert that back to the original with the same transpositions. Bars **7–8** have a 4-note chromatic line (adding one note to our motif but in retrograde inversion (upside down and backwards). The final D7+5 gives us our first hearing of the augmented 5th sound (this time on the dominant) later to be heard in the motif (augmented 5th of the tonic).

Initially I planned to go directly from the 8-bar piano intro to the head (melody chorus), but in performance it felt good to let the piano play a chorus first to set up the groove. This is common in the Basie style and was central to Thad Jones' post-Basie band. The problem that arises out of giving musicians solos before they play the head is that if they don't know the piece, their solo may not have anything to do with the motifs and spirit of the chart and therefore work against the arranger. In a working band such as ours, this piece has been played hundreds of times, so our excellent (and extremely intuitive) pianist, Isaac ben Ayala, knew exactly what I needed with no instructions other than, "Solo."

It is every soloist's duty to complete the arranger's job. This goes for the rhythm section as well.

Jimmy Hamilton told me that Duke Ellington didn't write chord changes for the soloists. The instrumental parts would just say, "Solo 32 bars," or something like that. On several occasions Jimmy asked Duke to write out the changes for him. Duke's response was, "If I do that, then you'll play all that stuff you practice. I want you to play my music." Similarly, Monk was known to have told his musicians, "Just play my song."

Rehearsal Letters vs. Bar Numbers

Notice that I use letters every 8 measures or so, rather than measure numbers. I find measure numbers on every bar distracting—too many extraneous black marks on the page. The players don't need to know this information and will have to avoid it while they look for the pitches and rhythms. Putting a letter every 8 bars or so will be enough for rehearsal purposes. Make sure that the letters (accompanied by double bars) occur on the first measure of sections. This reinforces the players' understanding of the form, and where their figures lie within the form. I prefer letters over numbers because, during a performance, if I want to cue a section (if someone or everyone is lost or to skip ahead or go back), I can make the sign of the letter with my fingers. This would be cumbersome with numbers above 10.

Computer copying programs include bar numbers on every measure as a default. As I said, I don't like to see bar numbers on parts or scores. I recommend turning off this option.

[Listen to **1-2: Piano Intro & Solo (mm1-E)**. The piano solo comes before the head and serves as a second intro. When you get to the end of the 8-bar intro, do you have a strong desire to continue listening and find out what this piece is all about? How about at the end of the piano chorus? Was Isaac successful in whetting your appetite? We won't really be able to assess the effectiveness of the intro until we have heard the entire arrangement. Only then will we know if the piece answers all the intro's questions. Was the intro specific enough? Did it get to the essence of the piece without giving away the ending?]

The Head

This riff-oriented melody is an exercise in how much a riff can be repeated without becoming boring or irritating. And furthermore—when we must get off the riff, how minimal a change can be made from our riff.

The form of the head is *abab'*, with each section being 8 measures. Starting with the sax pick-up into **E**, they play the riff four times, then twice transposing up a 4th (on the subdominant) and once another step higher (on the dominant) ending on a B (the 3rd of the key of G). The phrase is extended by going around the cycle of 5ths (B, E, A, D). The D is the first note of the original riff and starts the second half of the melody.

The first 11 bars of the second half are identical to the first 11 of the first half. Then the melody repeats the riff's rhythm but, instead of ascending chromatically, we descend down the tonic arpeggio (B, G, D). Descending by arpeggio is the opposite of ascending by steps. Nothing is more surprising and delightful than presenting an opposite.

Next, we have a series of six half notes: D, D#, E (our riff pitches), up a 5th to B, back down to E, E#, F# (the riff up a step). There is a quarter, half, quarter syncopation in the last bar of **H**. This is a shifting of gears. On the next bar it feels like we are going faster, but we're not. This effect is accomplished by having the drummer shift from the hi-hat to the ride cymbal, and by everyone modulating up a half step to A♭.

Chord Progressions: Melody/Bass Relationship

The chord progression of this tune is purposely simple. I always strive to have a strong melody/bass relationship. Those two parts should sound complete when played simultaneously. I first learned this from my study of Bach chorales in childhood. This concept was reinforced some years later when Chuck Israels told me that this was at the center of Bill Evans' harmonic language.

Once these outside parts are strong, the inside parts and countermelodies will fall into place easily. What makes the riff work is that while the melody stays the same, the chords change underneath, so we constantly hear the melody from a different perspective.

The first 8 bars are basically *I V I*. The top note of the riff (E) is the 6th of the G chord and the 9th of the D7. I learned how precious 6ths and 9ths can be from listening to Lester Young. I dressed things up a bit by using a couple of G#⁰ chords to smooth out the transition from the tonic (G) to the dominant (D7). The bassist will go from the G#⁰ to an A on the bottom of the D7 chords. Then he can either ascend or descend to the D on the next bar of the D7. This implies an Am7 D7 without stating it.

The second 8 bars of the melody take us to the subdominant and then cycles back to the dominant on the semi-cadence. The melody has moved up a 4th so that the A is now the 9th of the G7 and the 6th of the C. Notice the reverse order from the first 4 bars of letter **E**. When the melody then moves up a step to B, that becomes the 9th of the A7. Then it goes to E (the 5th of the A7). I could have gone directly to a D7 for the last 2 bars of this section, but that seemed too direct (I wanted just a little tease here), so I delayed the semi-cadence for a bar by going to the *ii7* (Am7) and then approaching the D7 from a half step above (E♭7). This is especially nice since the saxes are sitting on an A (the +11 of E♭7)—introducing a taste of some richness.

Since the melody of the next 11 bars is the same as the first 11 of letter **A**, I kept the harmony the same as well. Things get more interesting and chromatic from here on. This helps to set up the shifting of gears at the top of the next chorus. These last 4 bars are basically two different *iii vi ii V* turnarounds. In order to accommodate the chromatic melody, I used a B♭m7 in the first one and an E7-9 and A7 in the second.

Note also that I preceded the first turnaround with an F7 (the dominant of the upcoming B♭m7). The descending G arpeggio in the melody makes an upper structure triad over the F7 (+11, 9, 13). If all these relationships weren't good enough, there's one more nice one: the F7 is a 5th below the previous C6. The strong root movement makes this chord sound perfectly natural. It's the ♭*VII7* which is the common substitute for the *ivm* (Cm).

I love both those chords. They are so interchangeable that I always have to figure out which is better for each situation. In general I think of the *ivm* as an older sound, and the ♭*VII7* as more bebop, but this can vary depending on the melody and surrounding chords. The *ivm* feels sad to us, while the ♭*VII7* is more sophisticated than sad.

[Listen to **1-3: Head (E-I)** with attention to the chord progression and melody/bass relationship. Better yet, play through it on the piano and get the feel in your body. Jazz is very sensual. Music therapists say that the positive vibrations of soothing music massage the water molecules in our bodies.]

Orchestration

Now let's go back and look at the orchestration of this chorus. The bass and piano are given chord changes. The bass is free to walk. When Ellington was asked about how much information he gave the bassist, he said, "As little as possible." I will extend that to writing for every instrument. Only write information that the player does *not* know. Don't crowd the page with accents, longs, shorts, dynamics, etc. that are obvious idiomatic conventions.

Know for whom you are writing, and tailor the part to them. Make sure you leave room for them to interpret your music and breathe life into it. I love to control things as much as the next guy, but the purpose of my music is not to hear perfect reproductions of the sounds in my head. My music is meant to inspire the musicians to be great. When I hand them their parts, it becomes *their* music, and I am a coach and sometimes a referee, but never a dictator.

The Rhythm Section

The pianist should accompany the melody at **A** and stay out of the way of the harmonized brass figures when they begin. A common misconception that pianists have is that they should play the brass figures with the brass. This takes the bite out of the brass, and conflicts with their intonation and attacks. Look for the holes and answer the figures in the horns. Listen to Ellington and Basie. They knew how to make their bands sound great.

At **A** the drummer is instructed to play time on the hi-hat for this chorus. He can vary the pattern at will. When we perform this chart, our drummer, Jimmy Madison, likes to get his Sonny Payne/Basie groove on and play the ride pattern with closed hi-hat for the piano solo chorus and then the typical open/closed hi-hat pattern when the saxes enter. This keeps things intimate for the piano and then builds for the saxes. The switch to the ride cymbal at the modulation gives an even greater lift.

Besides keeping time, the drummer's next responsibility to the listener and the band is to define the form and make it easier for us to understand. He can do this in a number of ways. The most common are by switching cymbals for a new section or by setting up a new section with a rhythmic fill.

Texture

At **E** the saxes are in unison for 30 bars before they go into harmony. Many arrangers (especially beginners) shy away from unisons, thinking that the music will sound uninteresting and empty. If the rhythm and melody/bass relationship is good, it's already interesting. My own music is about 50% unison or solo, which is in keeping with Ellington, Strayhorn, Wynton Marsalis, Neal Hefti, Sy Oliver and just about every other arranger I like. The percentage of unison and solos will vary from piece to piece.

There are three basic textures: solo, unison and harmonized. There are many varieties of each of the three. Normally unisons are played without vibrato. Ellington called that "dead tone." Harmonized passages are played with or without vibrato depending on the style. When Ellington wanted vibrato, he would say to the horn players, "Give me some personality."

Unison in the horns allows the pianist some space to comp harmonies and also invites unison or harmonized counterpoint. We never (well, hardly ever) harmonize more than one idea at a time. That is confusing to the listener. The human ear is amazing, but it has its limitations. I never want to frustrate my audience. Tease, yes. Frustrate, no.

In my band I employ five reeds (2 alto saxes, 2 tenor saxes and one baritone sax. The lead alto doubles on soprano. All five double on flute and clarinet. We also have four bass clarinets, an alto flute, piccolo and bassoon when needed. On special occasions I will ask them to bring extra baritones, tenors, altos or sopranos. We get a lot of mileage out of those five guys), four trumpets (they can all play flugelhorn, but I generally only write it on the third part—I love Irv's flugelhorn sound and conception), three tenor trombones (doubles include tuba and euphoniums), piano, bass and drums. We usually employ a female singer, and occasionally a male singer. Seven of the horn players sing as well, and the entire band can participate in band vocals, whooping and hollering, clapping and stomping and added percussion when needed. We have on occasion added guitar, horn, cello and bass trombone for special projects. For large projects we have used choirs (from 50 up to 200 voices) and symphony orchestras.

Contrasting Characters

Getting back to our head (letters **E** through **H**), the trombones wait 12 measures before they answer the saxes, alternating chords with unisons. As a general rule, I keep the trombones off the unison sax melody notes. This gives the melody and accompaniment different characters. Note that the trombones are voiced around middle C. This is their most effective tessitura. Occasionally they go a little higher or a bit lower—but keep in mind that as they go above a third ledger line G, they get brighter but less powerful, and as they get lower in the bass clef, they lose brightness and punch. Trombones are tenor instruments, not bass instruments. If you want bass, use a bass trombone or a tuba.

The Use of Roots in Voicings

Notice that I do not use roots in any of the voicings in these 3 bars. The bassist is playing the roots, so we don't need to reinforce that in the brass. You'll also notice that sometimes I use roots and sometimes I don't. Roots give a fatter bottom and more firm footing. Some passages will have all the voicings with roots, some will be completely rootless and some will alternate. Listen to how they sound.

Placing the root on the bottom of a chord makes us feel like we are planting our foot on the ground, while using an inversion feels like we are lifting our foot up in the air. Given jazz's dance impulse, this is an important concept to embrace. Balance is important, just as it is with tension and release.

The weight of a voicing is determined by the distance from the top note to the bottom note. The wider the distance, the greater the weight.

If I use a root in a voicing, it is either in the bottom voice or the top voice, but rarely in an inside voice. If I use the root in an inside voice it is for one of these three reasons:

1. Part of a triad or upper structure triad *(Example 1-2)*.

2. For intervallic reasons—to create a 2nd, a tritone, 4th, etc. for dissonance or character or to create a good intervallic relationship between two parts *(Example 1-3)*.

3. For melodic reasons—to create a good melody in an inner part *(Example 1-4)*.

Voice Leading

I'm concerned with voice leading—that is, the melodies of the voices below the top part. Every horn player should have a melody that he will enjoy playing and that sounds good with the bass, the top part and all the other parts. This will give your music integrity, and when the cats enjoy playing your music, they will play it better. Not only will they be able to play their parts with authentic style and ease, you won't have to pay them as much as the other bands they work with. (Don't tell the other leaders that I told you this.)

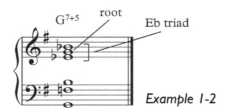

Example 1-2

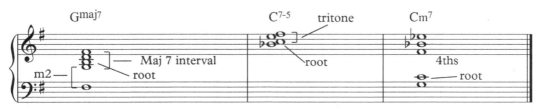

Example 1-3

Example 1-4

Voicing the Brass

Let's look at the two brass voicings in measure **F7**. Each voice descends by half step—chromatic approach (also called chromatic planing). This is standard procedure and will generally sound good, except when it doesn't. One reason it might not sound good is that it has become predictable, and it's time for a surprise. Notice that the trombones have the 3rd, 5th and 7th of the chord and the trumpets have the upper structures (+9, 13th and root). This sort of relationship between the trumpets and trombones is customary, but sometimes I like to vary it, as we shall see later on.

Call-and-response

On the second half of the head (**G** and **H**), the trombones take a more active role and engage in call-and-response with the saxes—each section is unison. Since the saxes are emphasizing the 6ths and 9ths of the chords, I give the bones the 3rds and 7ths with lower neighbors. While the sax riff repeats identically for 8 bars, the trombone riff repeats rhythmically with slight melodic variations before it departs in **G7–8**. Then it's back to the original rhythm in the bones, with pitches that reflect the new chord changes. After that, the bones play harmonized rhythmic jabs like a pianist's left hand for 2 bars before going back to unison. Keep in mind at all times the relationship of sameness and difference. This is at the root of all the arts, and especially humor.

Counterpoint

You can study European Classical counterpoint (and I have), but it all boils down to writing strong interdependent melodies. That means that both (or all, in the case of more than 2-part counterpoint) voices should be melodies that can stand on their own, but they also must have the special relationship of fitting hand and glove with each other. Basi-cally give each part different rhythms and different melody notes.

That way we can clearly hear each and understand them even when they are speaking at the same time. I recommend playing and studying the Bach inventions and fugues.

Sax Voicings

The saxophone voicings in **H7** to the downbeat of **H8** are quite ordinary. What makes them sound good is the motivic reference in the lead alto and the contrary and oblique motion between parts. When the bari and 4th Tenor play in 5ths, they are playing the same fingering, but their respective sizes place them a 5th apart. The overtones that are produced by the same fingerings are sympathetic. Sometimes when they are sitting next to each other, and they lock into 5ths, they will turn slightly towards each other and raise their eyebrows. It must be a saxophone thing. Brass players would never do that.

Smooth Modulation

This melody chorus ends on the downbeat of **H8**. We expect to hear a D7 on the third beat, but instead, there is a surprise dramatic quarter-half-quarter syncopation. The D7 is replaced with a D diminished that moves chromatically up to an E♭7 (the dominant of Ab). This modulates smoothly into the key of Ab; the D diminished being the pivot chord.

Wrong Note Voicing

The D root of the D diminished chord is the dominant in G (dominants are extremely strong) and the D diminished is the #IV° which moves up to V in A♭. The four lower parts in the saxes spell a D diminished in root position, however the top note (lead alto) is an E♭. The minor 9th interval between the lead alto and the bari is is extremely dissonant. Many people would consider it a wrong note. Why does it sound correct? The strong diatonic melody of 5, 3, 1 in the upcoming key of A♭ is so obvious that although we don't understand the initial E♭ when it is sounded, we think, "What is that?" and then three beats later, we understand the context. This is sometimes called a wrong note voicing. Jazz players play things like this all the time, but most jazz composers and arrangers tend to shy away from them. We need to encourage creativity.

[Time to pause and reflect on the head. There was a ton of information. This is the exposition of the piece, where the character is established. I suggest reading this section of the arrangement in 8-bar sections, and listening to each section before going on to the next: **1-4: (E-F), 1-5: (F-G), 1-6: (G-H),** and **1-7: (H-I)**. Then listen to it all together a few times, **1-3: Head (E-I)** until you have digested all the relationships. I realize that this is very challenging.

Many years ago Wynton Marsalis and I used to analyze Duke Ellington's scores like this; sometimes in my apartment, sometimes on planes or in airports when we were on the road. Wherever we were, we always were amazed at the depth of the construction of the Maestro's music. Even music that seemed simple had complex relationships, and conversely, even the most complex music had an underlying simplicity.

Keep in mind that neither Ellington nor I was aware of all, or even most of, these relationships and reasons for writing this note or that while we were in the process of writing. The great tenor saxophonist, Sal Nistico, once said to me, "You are playing your best when you don't know what you are doing." Of course

Sal was assuming that before you got up to play, you had spent 10,000 hours learning the language of the greats and gaining technical proficiency on your instrument. When he said that you don't know what you are doing, he meant that your conscious (logical) mind was letting your subconscious (intuitive) mind take over.]

Solos, Solis and Shout Choruses

Most jazz arrangements (small and big band) post-New Orleans use a form that roughly corresponds to Sonata Allegro form:

> *Introduction*
> *Exposition*
> *Development*
> *Recapitulation*
> *Coda.*

The head is our exposition. Our development can consist of solos (with or without backgrounds), solis and shout choruses. All of these three components can be optional and depend on the nature and direction of each individual arrangement. **Stompin' On A Riff** has two solo choruses (alto and trumpet), a shout chorus (16 bars soft and 16 bars loud). No solis.

Backgrounds

The purpose of background figures is to accompany and guide the soloist; make it easy for him to create a solo that will fit the arrangement. Try to keep it simple—an accompaniment, not competition, for him.

Listen to the great piano accompanists: Ellington, Horace Silver, Hank Jones, John Lewis, Sonny Clark, Roland Hanna, et al. Notice how they feed the soloist without pushing him into a corner. The best accompanists will develop motivic ideas. When I write for horns, I often orchestrate things I have heard pianists play either in their comping or solos, so that the horns take over the pianist's function. Chuck Israels told me that he once asked the wonderful pianist Bill Dobbins to comp in a more motivic and creative manner. Bill responded, "Oh, you mean more like a big band?" Funny how one thing influences the other and comes full circle like instrumentalists trying to sound more like vocalists and then vocalists trying to emulate instrumentalists.

You'll notice that all the figures under the solos and all the figures in the shout chorus develop from our 3-note motif. This gives the piece unity and character. For me, it is fun to see how much mileage I can get out of an idea.

The general rule for backgrounds is to accompany a solo with an opposing color, to avoid having the listener being confused between foreground and background.

As established by the early jazz arrangers like Don Redman and Fletcher Henderson, brass solos are generally accompanied by reed backgrounds and vice versa. There are other ways to differentiate: different mutes, different registers, different dynamics, different speeds, etc.

Trumpet Solo with Backgrounds

Let's take a look at the relationship of foreground and background for the trumpet and alto sax solos. The plunger trumpet solo at **I** starts with call-and-response between the harmonized saxes and the unison three remaining trumpets in plungers in their low register (below where the soloist will be playing). Because we have modulated up a half step to the key of Ab, our motif is no longer D, D#, E, but is now Eb, E♮, F. The retrograde is F, E, Eb (the pitches in the lead alto from **I1** through **I6**).

The Tritone

There is one added note in the alto—C♭. C♭ is a tritone, or half an octave away from F. In jazz we frequently use tritone substitution in our harmonies (and jazz musicians love to talk about them all the time), but that same relationship of dividing the octave in half is also true melodically. Every note of the scale has a somewhat equal relationship with its tritone.

Blue Notes

There are two other important relationships at work for that C♭. C♭ is a blue note in the key of Ab. The three blue notes are b3, b5 and b7. C♭ is the b3. Blue notes establish a feeling of jazz. They can be in the melody, background, countermelody or inside parts.

The third and most important reason for this usage of the C♭ is that it acknowledges the opposing trumpet line in the call-and-response, but because of its rhythmic placement, it doesn't agree with it. The agreement comes 2 bars later in the trumpets.

Justification

The trumpets have a repeated riff figure at **I** that answers the sax downbeats and anticipated downbeats. They play two pitches (C♭, Ab) six times while the harmonies change in the saxes and rhythm section. When we hear the first C♭, we question, why C♭? When it is followed by the tonic (Ab), it is apparent that we are establishing the new key of Ab and a relationship with the blues. We accept this for a while, but keep wondering what this has to do with the 5 #5 6 motif of this piece.

Just when we are about to write off this guy Berger as a superficial arranger who leaves loose ends, the C♭ is enharmonically respelled B♮ and the line moves up chromatically to an

Eb. This is our motive transposed down a 3rd and extended by two more half steps just to rub your doubt in your face. And isn't it nice how that last Eb agrees with the lead alto's final Eb? By the way, notice the chromatic movement in the inside parts in the saxes. More motivic stuff, but the best is the last four notes of the bari: Eb E♮ Gb F. It's our motif with an added chromatic upper neighbor (Gb F).

The relationship of background and foreground is present between the top part of a harmonized passage and the inside parts.

I tried to keep the backgrounds from becoming too notey, so they wouldn't hamper the soloist, who will probably be playing mostly eighths and quarters. Recognizing that letter **B** is on the busy side for a background, letter **J** offers a respite for the first 6 bars. The saxes continue with their 5-part harmony, but now they play long legato notes rather than short staccato. We love the drama of opposites.

Take a look at the lead alto melody at **J**: 5, #5, 6 (our motif), b3 (our old friend from letter **I**) and then a 5-note chromatic motif starting on the tonic (Ab) and ending on the 3rd (C). This gives new meaning to the Cb—it is the enharmonic leading tone to the C. In case you missed the significance of this statement of the motif, the saxes repeat the final note and add accents and a syncopation in **J5**. Again notice how the inside parts move so smoothly in mostly half steps creating different versions of the motif.

6-part Brass Voicings

The brass takes over from the saxes in **J7** and **8**, but they reverse the order of long and short. Incidentally this rhythm is a condensed (2-bar) version of the 4-bar rhythmic figure in the saxes at **I**. The six brass (open—the plung-

ers are removed) are voiced in 6-part harmony with as little doubling as possible. We saw this sort of thing in the sax voicings. Each voice has its own pitch. This feels individualistic. In the case of the two brass voicings, the roots appear in both the top and bottom parts. None of the other parts double. The lead trumpet is in a comfortable mid-range so as not to overly distract us from the trumpet solo.

Inversion and Retrograde

Notice how there is no 11th (Eb) in the Bbm7, nor is there a 9th (F) in the Eb7 in the brass. You will find those pitches in the unison sax line, which just happens to be our motif followed by both the inversion or retrograde transposed a half step higher. Be aware that the inversion and the retrograde are one and the same for completely chromatic passages: Eb, E, F becomes F, E, Eb. Also notice that the rhythm in the saxes on this unison is the retrograde of their rhythm in **J5** but repeated twice.

More Call-and-response with an Evolving Motif

Letter **K** returns to the call-and-response pattern from **I**, but with a variation in the saxes and with the trombones replacing the trumpets. The lead alto has 5, b3, 2, 2, 3, 6. Starting and ending with 5, 6 is a 2-note version of our motif. b3, 2, 3 is b6, 5, 6 transposed up a 5th to the dominant. This is our motif with the middle pitch moved ahead of the first pitch. Changing the order is a great developmental technique. We recognize it as the motif, but know that it is evolving. The key is to make motivic changes gradually, so the listener can follow your logic.

The trombones respond in unison (the opposite of the harmonized saxes) on repeated Eb's (the dominant). The trombones are agreeing with the lead alto's first note and continuing to insist on it even while the saxes move on to other things. The E♭ also relates back to the previous trumpet answers at **I** that kept returning to the tonic. The trombones have a low A natural in the middle of their second answer. This is related to the E♭ by tritone.

The first 4 bars at **L** are a development of **J7** and **8**, only now it's just the harmonized trombones filling in harmonies where the sax unison rests or holds a pitch. Notice how the bones avoid the sax notes. This makes it easier for the listener to distinguish between foreground and background. The unison tonics (A♭'s) in **L2** are the resolution of the previous dominants in letter **K**.

The unison sax line at **L** is the motif twice and then the motif up a 4th. The final C starts as the major 7th of D♭, then becomes the −5 of G♭7 and finally resolves to the 3rd of the tonic A♭ chord (which establishes that we have ultimately arrived home after an interesting trip). The unison trumpets (returning to plungers and fanning open and closed) hammer away at the dominant, further establishing our solid tonality in case there was any doubt. The bone voicings occur in the rhythmic holes of the trumpet rhythms and avoid the trumpet pitches as well.

Tutti Writing

Total agreement comes to all the horns in the last 2 bars of this chorus (**L7–8**). This is written in classic tutti style. I start with 4-way close (block) voicings from the top down in the brass. Since there are 6 brass (one of the trumpets has just finished his solo and needs at least 8 bars to open his eyes, return to his seat and switch gears from soloing back into playing his role in the section), the bottom

two trombones will double the top two trumpets down the octave.

This being a mid-range tutti with only four saxes available (the lead alto is about to start his solo in the next measure, so he needs time to close his eyes, stand up and switch gears into the world of improvisation), the saxes double the brass from the second voice down. That means the following doubles: Reed 2/Tpt 3, Reed 3/Tpt 4, Reed 4/Tbn 1, Reed 5/Tbn 2 (Tpt 1 8vb). Trombone 3 is by himself (Tpt 3 8vb). Note that the bari doubles the 1st Trumpet down the octave. This octave doubling of the brightest instrument and the darkest instrument warms up the ensemble sound.

The trumpets are open for this tutti passage. The first measure (**L7**) in the lead trumpet is the riff formerly played in plunger an octave below in the first measure of this chorus. How pleasing to reprise it and tie up the package with a nice ribbon and bow! Let's not stop there. Let's do it again, but before we do, let's utilize another blue note (the ♭5), resolve that down by half-step (a 2-note inversion/retrograde version of our motif) and voice it with diminished chords. The melody notes are all a half step below the chord tones of the diminished, creating a major 7th interval with the fourth harmony part.

[Listen to **1-8: Trumpet Solo (I-M)**, with its backgrounds. For what seems to be a simple accompaniment, there is a lot going on. Every member of the band is integral here and throughout the piece.]

Alto Solo with Backgrounds

The tutti voicings ending the trumpet solo overlap the choruses and continue 3 bars into the alto solo chorus. The lead trumpet has 5, 6, ♭3, 5, 6—the 2-note motif with the tritone

(♭3) in the middle. I relieved the static tonic chord with a ♭II7 resolving back to the tonic (although only in the rhythm section). That is followed with a passing A°, which resolves to a B♭m7 and finally to an E♭9. I used the B♭m7 rather than going directly to the E♭7 to give some motion between the two chords in **M3**.

Saxes in Drop 2 Voicings

After the horns take a well-needed breath for six beats, the four remaining saxes play a half note line in classic Drop 2 spacing for 7 bars. The top part goes up the diatonic scale 4, 5, 6, 7 (a diatonic variation of our motif with an added step) before descending 6, ♭6, 5, 4, 3, 2 (inversion/retrograde with continued diatonic scale notes added). When the saxes slow down from their half notes to hold out longer notes, the bones answer in unison with 6, 5, 1 and then extend that one more note to 6, 5, 1, ♭3—retrograde 2-note motif with the added tonic and then added blue note.

Personal Expression

The trumpets and saxes answer the bones with repeated 7-part harmony pecks opposing bone answers on unison dominants. The saxes are voiced below the trumpets with the top alto overlapping the bottom trumpet and repeating our happy note, the 6th. The saxes jump right back in with their Drop 2 long note in **N7–8**. They enter with a smear to give some expression.

Here is a case where I knew that I would need a smear. I generally don't indicate most embellishments, and leave them up to the players. Players like to have the opportunity to be creative, and also don't like to feel that they are in a straitjacket. Not only did Duke Elllington not indicate inflections or embellishments in his music, he didn't even write dynamics. I write some dynamics, but leave most to the discretion of the players, so they can find themselves in the music.

Chromatic Approach

O2 is the same as **L7**. Both measures have the same chord progression (A♭ A°). The lead trumpet in **O3** starts like **L8** but down a half step and then resolves down to the root of the dominant chord. I used chromatic approach (half step planing) for the first two chords (E13 E♭13). The E13 is an 8th note on the downbeat. It goes by quickly. I didn't want to disrupt the groove in the rhythm section, so I didn't tell them about it.

Augmented 5ths

The voicing for the final chord of **O3** is an E♭7+5. I augmented the 5th to add some motion rather than repeat the diatonic notes of the previous E♭13. This was a standard procedure in the 1920s and 30s. Notice the pitches in Trumpet 1 for **O2–3** (C♭, A♭, D♭, C, E♭). If you remove the A♭ and E♭ (tonic and dominant), you are left with C♭, D♭, C—our motif transposed up a minor 6th with the second note first. Two of the three inside parts are also transpositions (up a minor 3rd and up a 5th). The remaining inside part is our motif (E♭, E, F) slightly altered to E♭, G♭, F, so that the middle note resolves chromatically downwards to the final note instead of upwards. I also like the chromatic resolution of the inserted C to B♮ in that part.

Re-harmonization

More chromatics appear in the first three notes of **O6–7**, but harmonized differently. The lead trumpet's B♮, C, B♭ is the out of order inversion/retrograde transposed up a 5th. The C is harmonized as the 13th of an E♭7.

The preceding chord (not represented in the rhythm section) is an E9, so that the top part moves up chromatically while the other three parts descend by half step. The contrary motion sets up the resolution to the tonic in a dramatic way. The tonic chord on the downbeat of **O7** is an Ab69 with the 9th in the melody. Notice how every part moves stepwise in a motivic manner. It is very satisfying for musicians to play logical and motivic melodic parts inside the voicings.

Blue Notes on Major 6th Chords

An interesting thing happens in **O7-8**: repeated Eb's (dominants) in a band unison lead to a couple of Gb's alternating with Eb's. The Gb's are blue notes. This is not an Ab7. This is clearly Ab6 with b7 blue notes. Now that this concept is introduced, I'm going to start developing more along these lines.

Contrary Motion on Climaxes

Here are the lead trumpet pitches for **P1-2**: Ab, Eb, Eb, F, Fb, Eb, Ab. Although I am voicing this as a tutti, the first and last notes (both Ab's) are unison. The second, third and fourth notes are our motif, and the fourth, fifth and sixth notes are the inversion or retrograde. I voiced the Eb as an Ab9 and the E as an A9. I could have continued with parallel harmony up and down, but I voiced the F as the 13th of an Ab13 and then back to A9 Ab9. This creates contrary motion on the top note of the phrase—something I frequently do. In this case, it draws attention to this mini-climax.

Harmonizing Blue Notes

P3 is similar to **O8**—alternating between the blue note and the 5th. In this case we are in 4-part harmony, so I can't just imply it like before. I harmonized the Ab's as Db6 chords and

the Cb's as D13's. The third voice down has repeated E naturals—the 9th of D13 and the +9 of Db6. 6th chords with +9's are unusual but can be quite evocative.

Using Tensions on the Tops of Voicings

The lead trumpet in **P4–6** is Ab, Eb, Ab, Eb, Eb, F–tonic, dominant, tonic and then our motif. Notice how all but the second note (Eb) are tensions of the chords: 9, 5, +9, 11, -9, 13. Also notice how chromatic and motivic every part is for all of letter **P**. The six beats of rest in **P7–8** allow the rhythm section to diminuendo into a soft shout chorus.

[Listen to **1-9: Alto Solo (M-Q)**. These backgrounds are more active than during the previous trumpet solo. We are definitely building. There is more rhythmic punch and the melodies are more chromatic, but the textures are all simple—either 4-way close or unison.

I reiterate: I was not consciously thinking of the minutiae that I have just described. Mostly I just write what I hear and what sounds good to me at that moment. The question is: why does one thing sound good to me while another thing does not?

When I was in high school, either my music sounded to me like my heroes' music or it didn't. It was hit or miss; trial and error. As I grew, I analyzed music that I liked and applied the same standards to my music. Just being conscious got me to the next level of artistry—that, and the desire to write the best music I could every time I put pencil to paper.]

The Shout Chorus

The shout chorus is where everything comes together. It's the climax—what we have been working towards and where it finally explodes. Sometimes (and this is one of those times) we like a bit more of a tease and start with a soft shout (oxymoron, I know) and then proceed to a loud shout (usually with a drum fill transition between them). Two very famous examples of soft/loud shout choruses are Frank Foster's *Shiny Stockings* and Ernie Wilkins' *Corner Pocket* (both written for and recorded by the Count Basie New Testament Band of the 1950s). That band also recorded Neal Hefti's *Splanky*. *Splanky* doesn't have a soft shout, but I had to mention it, because it might be the greatest shout chorus in all of jazz.

All three of these charts are required listening for everyone in the universe. They express the joy we feel being alive. I have performed these three charts hundreds of times (maybe even thousands of times), and every time when we get to the loud shout chorus, I can feel everyone in the place (band and audience, dancers, bartenders, waitresses, everyone) on the same beat, release the tension in their bodies and forget everything in their lives except for the absolute ecstasy of the moment. Or as Woody Allen once said, "It's the most fun I ever had with my clothes on."

When you know these three pieces, you will know what to shoot for. Of course every piece is different, and every climax is different. The word climax implies sex, and there are obvious parallels: foreplay, teasing, build up, climax, smoking the cigarette (we don't do that anymore—now we cuddle). Sex is different with each partner and even different each time with the same partner if we are creative. I know arrangers who write the same chart over and over, and I know others who never do the same thing twice. I try to find the uniqueness in every situation; be it musical or interpersonal. I may be mostly the same person, but the music is different and other

people are different. The more I explore *them* and the less I try to impose control, the more creative I can be.

Key changes (modulations) create important formal structure.

In traditional march form (which was appropriated for rags and traditional New Orleans music) there is a short modulation to the key of the subdominant just prior to the trio section. Whenever I hear a change of key (not just a temporary one within the form of the song), it signals a new section in a powerful but subtle way. Most jazz arrangements (big band and small group) do not change key. We just add chorus after chorus creating new melodies over the structure of the harmonies.

This works in most cases, but sometimes (especially if the song's harmonies are simple) we need a lift. It's become a cliche, but many vocal arrangements modulate up a half step for the last chorus. Ella Fitzgerald's arrangement of *Mack The Knife* goes up a half step every chorus, and we all know how exciting that is!

If we look at the form (see above—near the beginning of this chapter), it's easy to see how the modulations define the form: intro and melody chorus in G, solos in A♭, shout in E♭ then B♭ and recap and coda in the original key of G. To be perfectly honest, the only key that was planned was the modulation back to G for the recap. I wanted it to feel like we are returning home after a long journey. This is not a novel idea. Sonata Allegro form has been returning to the original key for over 200 years.

Where modulating to the key of the dominant is commonplace in Classical Music, jazz musicians and classic American songs rarely do this. Mostly they modulate to the key of the subdominant. Step-wise modulations are the next most common (especially in vocal arrangements where the singer's range is limited) followed by 3rd related keys. I chose the keys for this arrangement simply because that is where I heard the melody going. At those moments I felt the need for a subtle lift. It turned out that each one is quite effective, so my intuition was right. Or was it? Let's see.

Wrong Turns, Missing the Turn and Good Sex

The first draft of the chart had a trombone solo in E♭ following the alto solo (in place of what is now the shout chorus) and then went directly to the recap in G. When the band read it down at a rehearsal, I knew immediately that this wasn't going to work, and that I needed to lengthen the trumpet and alto solos (they were originally a half chorus each) and move directly to the shout. As I said before, I often hear arrangements where I feel like we are driving down the highway and the guy behind the wheel isn't paying attention and misses the exit sign. This happens more in music than it does on the highway—and it happens plenty on the highway.

Getting back to our sexual analogy, a good lover just knows how much foreplay and teasing are enough, and when it's time to push to the climax. The greatest example in jazz of a parallel to the sexual experience is Ellington's 1946 arrangement of *Rockin' In Rhythm,* which he performed almost every day until his death

28 years later. Even the title tells us what he was describing. If you don't know the version on ***The Great Paris Concert*** (1963) Atlantic Records, then you are in for a real treat. Not only is it deeply swinging, but everything happens at the perfect moment.

In order to keep some continuity, it's usually best not to change all the elements in the music when entering a new section—especially when modulating.

At **P8** I am modulating to a new key (E♭). I keep the rhythm and melody of our motif in their original form just adding one note at the end. The orchestration, harmony and voicings continue with the same 4-way close tutti. Besides the key change, other changes are: the drummer diminuendos and moves to closed hi-hat, the horns play subito piano, the alto sax stops soloing, and the pianist answers the horns with some light upper register Basie-like fills.

There are four basic types of modulation:

1. Abrupt (sudden), no preparation. The first note and chord are in the new key. Rarely used, but can be quite effective (and shocking). *(Example 1-5)*

2. Common tone—the last note of the old key is held over and becomes the first note of the new key. If we are in F major and modulate to D major, we could end on an Fmaj7 with the 3rd (A) in the melody, and then tie that A over while the harmony underneath changes to a Dmaj7. Effective, and not often used. *(Example 1-6)*

Example 1-5
Direct modulation

Example 1-6
Common tone

3. Sequential. Repeating the last figure, starting on a different pitch and continuing in the new key. *(Example 1-7)*

4. Prepared (smooth). The new key is set up by its dominant or chromatic upper or lower neighbor. The dominant can be preceded by a chord or chords that will take us seamlessly from the old key to the new one. There is generally a pivot chord that functions in both keys. 95% of modulations are of this type. *(Example 1-8)*

The modulation into letter **Q** is prepared. The pivot chord is the A°—it's both the #i° in A♭ major and the #iv° in E♭ major. Although the next chord (Fm7) could be heard as the vi of A♭ major and the ii of E♭ major, the bassist plays B♭'s on the bottom of the chord to clearly establish the dominant of E♭.

Motivic Development

The development of our motif hits its peak in the shout chorus. This is the arranger's moment to shine. The soloists and backgrounds have been moving the development along, but the bulk of the work is done here.

Tutti Writing

I've continued the tutti writing for the first 13 bars of the shout chorus. I could have scored it with open voicings and roots on the bottom, but that would be too heavy for a soft shout and wouldn't leave me anywhere to build to for the loud shout that follows. 4-part tutti writing doesn't have to be vanilla (bland).

Even though there is limited usage of prime dissonances (minor 2nd, major 7th, minor 9th) and the use of contrary motion, the motivic nature of the melody and underparts (voice leading) makes this interesting. It's not ultra-modern or avant garde, but it's not supposed to be. The purpose is to tease and set up the big shout.

Look at the lead trumpet part (which is also doubled an octave lower in the 1st Trombone and bari). Starting with the pick-up to **Q**, this is all about our motif. The first three notes are our motif in the new key (E♭). After that, the tonic (E♭) is sounded to establish the tonality and start a variation of the motif. If we start on the E♭ and omit the auxiliary pitches, we can boil these first 7 bars down to an upwardly moving scale line: E♭, F, F# and G. This is our motif transposed up a 5th with an added starting pitch.

Notice all the diatonic scale movement in the melody: from the tonic up to the 6th. This is the inversion (and also the retrograde) of the first interval at letter **Q**. The A♭, F#, G in **Q6–7** is the motif a minor 6th above the original, but out of order—the last note is first. The two final C's in **Q7** punctuate the end of the phrase by using the repeated high note (C), putting it down an octave—making it the lowest note of the phrase and repeating it for stress. To add emphasis, I put a blue note in the voicing (+9 in place of the root). This stands out as being the most dissonant voicing in the phrase (the F# rubs against the G).

Example 1-7
Sequential

Example 1-8
Prepared (smooth)

The voicings in this whole passage are simple 4-part 9th chords alternating with passing diminisheds in parallel motion, until we get to the cadence in **Q7**. Note the contrary motion from the F7-9 to the E7+9: the top part moves up chromatically while the other three parts descend chromatically. Contrary motion helps to establish the cadence.

The melody at letter **R** similarly has two different lines going on at the same time: our motif played twice (the rhythm is displaced the second time, but the pitches are the same), the tonic E♭ (like at **Q**, but this time up the octave), then a descending 5th (C, F) with repeated F's for emphasis (like **Q7**, but twice as fast), the motif down a step with two added diatonic pitches (going up the scale in similar fashion to **Q5–6**). The D becomes the top note of a descending 5th (a whole step higher than the descending 5th in **R3–4**).

At this point the piano and drums start their crescendo fills to usher in the shout chorus. The saxes come in a bar later to help the crescendo using the three C's as auxiliary notes (as in letter **Q**) and an altered 4-note version of the motif (A♭, G, E, F). The saxes are voiced in 4-way close with the lead doubled down the octave in the bari. The ensuing unison F's with the G♭ trill-like embellishment (a 2-note chromatic reduction of our motif) set up the dominant of the up-coming key of B♭.

The Loud Shout, Brass Voicings and Contrary Motion

The loud shout begins two beats early to incorporate our motif (5, #5, 6) in the new key (B♭). The brass is voiced in 7-part harmony. I always keep in mind that each section should make a good sonority within itself as well as combining with the other sections in a more dense chord—so the trumpets should sound good by themselves and the bones should sound good by themselves, and when they play together they will sound equally good, but with more pitches. Note how in some of the brass chords there are seven different pitches and other chords have one or two notes in the trumpets doubled down the octave in the trombones. At no time are notes doubled within a section. There are always 4 trumpet pitches (mostly tensions— 9th, 11th, 13th and altered tensions) and 3 trombone pitches (mostly chord tones—1,3,5,7) in each chord. This is pretty conventional.

Usually it is not good to double a trumpet and trombone in unison—although, octaves are fine), because the trombone will be in a much stronger register than the trumpet and it is hard to balance in volume and timbre. There is only one chord where the 1st Trombone doubles a trumpet voice at the unison. Those notes are arrived in contrary motion and are left in contrary motion. Contrary motion preserves the integrity of the individual lines. If we used parallel motion, it would sound (and feel) like one of the voices disappeared.

Let's take a look at the lead trumpet in **R8–S6**: our motive followed by a B♭, motif followed by B♮, motif followed by C, C#, D. All this adds up to the motif three times and an upwardly chromatic line from B♭ to D (or you could say that this is the motive down a 5th (same notes as in our previous key of E♭) and extended by two additional half steps.

Saxes vs. Brass, Unison vs. Voicings

While all this rich harmony and motivic development is going on in the brass, the saxes play a unison line in counterpoint to the brass. The altos and tenors are in prime unison and the bari is an octave below. This puts all the saxes in strong and comfortable registers on their instruments. The brass play predominantly long notes and rests, so in contrast the saxes play predominantly faster notes (8th notes) and rest when the brass are active. For the most part, the saxes avoid the lead trumpet notes. The only exception is the final G in **S5**. For that split second they are in agreement, and then they go back to arguing.

Developing the Motif

These 7 bars of sax unison are the most adventurous challenges to the motif we have heard so far. The 2-note variant of the motif (from **R8**) becomes the basis for **S1–3** happening on the 3rd, major 7th and 3rd, then repeating the 3rd and major 7th. One of the beautiful things about these figures is that the middle note (the chromatic lower neighbor) is always a blue note (either the $\flat3$ or $\flat7$). Remember the downward intervals of the 5th in the lead trumpet in **R2–5**? Those descending 5ths return now in the saxes in **S1–4** (D, A, D, G then D, A, G.

That last G also serves as the first note of our motif transposed up a step (G, G#, A). The A is the 3rd of the F7. The saxes arpeggiate 3, 5, 7, 9 landing on the G. The next two pitches are G#, A (our motif up a step again, but this time with a rest and octave displacement between the first two notes—G and G#). The following C and E$\flat$ complete the 3,5,7 arpeggio on F7. In essence **S3–6** is all F7. The other chords are merely passing chords to smooth things out and create a little resistance. So in **S6** the saxes are just playing F7 and ignoring the G$\flat$7 in the brass and rhythm section.

Beats 3 and 4 in **S6** and the downbeat of **S7** are a 4-note version of the motif with the first note displaced by an octave and the second note (G$\flat$) added as an upper neighbor to the fourth note (F). The F is the 5th of the B$\flat$

chord. The saxes arpeggiate up the triad and then land on 6, $\flat$6, 5 (the retrograde of the motif). That is followed by the tonic (to establish the key, just as before).

5-Part Sax Voicings

The saxes take over in harmony for 5 measures. The lead part starts with the motif up a 4th and then alternates between the first and third notes omitting the chromatic link between them. The voicings are all parallel using diminished sounds for the first 2 bars of **T**. The voicings have a 4th on top and all minor 3rds stacked below that.

Saxes and Brass in Tandem

In **T5–7** the saxes return to the 2-note variant from 8 bars earlier. This time they leave space for the brass on the *ands* of beats 2 and 4. Notice how the saxes hint at the chromaticism of the motif (G, E$\flat$, F, A$\flat$, D and A) while the brass interject their own variant (F, C, E$\flat$, G, F#, A, B$\flat$, D and A$\flat$). This is the wildest spot in the chart. Lots of tension is built up between the saxes and brass.

[Listen to **1-10: Shout Chorus (Q-U)**, and see if you can hear what I've been describing. You might want to just listen to a bar or two at one time. I get much more of the feel of a piece by playing it on the piano than I do by listening—you can play the voicings, or just take a line at a time in your right hand, while playing the root of the chord in your left. It's also fun to play combinations of two voices together.

Once again, I'll remind you that I wasn't thinking consciously about most of the things I've described. Once the first chorus of a chart is written, for me the rest of the chart pretty much writes itself. I let my subconscious mind take over and use my conscious logic to tidy up loose ends when needs be.

Bob Brookmeyer likened his writing process to being like a radio receiver. He didn't know where the music came from, but if he was tuned in properly, the music just flowed through him. Not everyone can adjust their radio dials as finely as Bob did. It takes a lot of talent, courage and hard work to be able to do that.]

The Recapitulation

The natural release for this tension is to go back to the simplest form of the motif in the original key (G). Instead of giving the theme to the saxes at **U** (as it was orchestrated in the exposition), the trombones take over. There are two reasons for this:

1. We just heard unison saxes and harmonized brass. It would be refreshing to reverse their roles.

2. The trombones will bring a little more personality and struggle to the part, and leave me the opportunity to do something more involved with the saxes.

Truncated Form

Rather than play the complete 32-bar form, I opted to shorten the form in order to focus on simple riffs on the tonic and dominant. This 8-bar section repeats three times, adding the trumpets and saxes. Finally, on the last time, the horns drop out, and the motif is played by the piano in the upper register (reducing the entire chart to its simplest element and reminding us of how the piano started

everything). An added bit of drama is to terrace the dynamics one level down for each repeat, which creates an effect like hearing a parade band march off down the street.

The trumpets play simple 4-way close voicings alternating closed and open with plungers. The 9ths and 13ths add some spice. When the saxes enter on the next repeat they play the motif starting on the 5th, 9th and 5th and then omitting the 9th, they play the final two notes (A#, B). Note that their accents coincide with the trumpets and oppose the trombones.

[Listen to **1-11: Recap (U)**. Get the feel of how it builds when we add sections with a contrapuntal idea and then how it comes way down with just the piano in the high register. Notice how the bones and trumpets oppose each other, and then the saxes tie them together. All three sections are speaking at the same time and creating an interesting and exciting tapestry, but we can easily hear each of them. This is the goal in contrapuntal writing.]

The Coda

The function of the coda is to give us a satisfying feeling of finality and leave us with an understanding of the scope of the piece. It's kinda like the intro in reverse. The time for new material is long past. That ended before the recapitulation.

The standard vaudeville tag ending starts on the subdominant and cycles back to the tonic *(Example 1-9)*.

I've used a variation of the chord progression to that tag. I start with a unison tonic pickup to letter **V** and then switch to ensemble

Example 1-9

voicings. Notice how the saxes are on the bottom (roots in the bari), bones and upper saxes around middle C and the trumpets on top. This gives the fattest sound. The 6-note lead trumpet melody presents three sets of 2-note variations of the motif: A#-B (second and third note), D-E (first and third note) and C-B (inversion or retrograde of the second and third note). The harmonies basically move around the cycle of 5ths using chord qualities that accommodate the melody notes rather than all the chords being dominant 7ths.

I avoided the Basie cliché signature ending (even though that would have been motivic) and opted to give the break to the harmonized trombones. They play the motif three times (twice in the original form and once down a step). The displaced rhythm pushes us into the final statement of the motif by the full ensemble. The contrary motion resolving into a 13+11 tonic chord announces the end of the piece in no uncertain terms—we have the motif and its inversion in several keys at the same time. The rhythm section puts the final nail in the coffin with a Charleston rhythm, which just happens to be the rhythm of our motif minus the middle note.

[Listen to **1-12: Coda**. Does it sum up the entire piece and feel satisfying? I love restating the motif in the coda. I've never had a problem ending pieces. Intros are intimidating to write, but endings come easily to me. I always try to do something different and tailor the ending to the piece at hand.

Duke Ellington often had trouble writing endings to his arrangements. He would improvise endings on the piano, let the musicians suggest or improvise endings *(Afro Bossa)* or assign endings to Billy Strayhorn *(Harlem, I Got It Bad)*. Duke's sister, Ruth, once told me that the Maestro had a fear of death and that endings symbolized death to him. Sounds a bit weird, but he was superstitious; among other things, he never wore green after 1935, because he was wearing a green suit on the day his mother died.]

Evaluation

[Listen once more to **1-1: Complete Arrangement**. Ask yourself the same three questions we asked in the beginning:

1. What do you like about this chart?
2. What don't you like?
3. How might you do it better?

How do your answers differ from before you read my analysis? Does the piece sound different to you now?]

Something very important to keep in mind:

The acid test for a piece of music is not how logical it is, but does it sound and feel satisfying?

A great piece of music must satisfy on both a visceral and intellectual level. Great art is great forever. If we aim high and miss, the results can still be pretty good. If our idols are less than great, the chances of us measuring up to the greats are slim, and so our efforts are limited. If we stand on the shoulders of giants and fall short, we still are doing pretty well.

The true joy in creating art is not in the final product, but in the process. The mere act of aspiring to greatness is both elevating and nourishing for the soul. Aspiring to mediocrity on the other hand is soul-crushing. If you want to really have fun, dare to dream big and live your dream. Take chances. In music the liabilities are minimal. Not all of my arrangements or performances were great, but as far as I know, no one ever died from one.

2. Hindustan

[At www.suchsweetthundermusic.com/pages/cjca-accompanying-files listen to **2-1: Complete Arrangement**. Now ask yourself these three questions that I ask myself whenever I listen to music:

1. What do you like about this chart?
2. What don't you like?
3. How might you do it differently?]

In art, imagination trumps fact.

Hindustan is a song written in 1918 by Oliver Wallace and Harold Weeks and is in the public domain. The title is an archaic term for the Indian sub-continent, evoking an exotic feeling of a part of the world that is as foreign to me as it was to the songwriters. Of course I've read all kind of books, seen movies and read the newspaper about such places, so I have a feeling for what it might be like.

I might be wrong, but that doesn't mean that the world that I create in my music isn't a good fantasy. When Duke Ellington created his world-famous "jungle music" at the Cotton Club in the 1920s, he had never been to Africa, or listened to African music. What he created was his version of African music that was based on American jazz—elevating some of the pseudo-African clichés of the day to fine art. After touring the Middle East 40 years later, he composed the **Far East Suite** (a misnomer to be sure). Again, he made no at-

tempt to reproduce authentic native music of that region. The original title of the suite was *Impressions Of The Far East.* I'm following in that tradition and having fun.

Finding a new angle from which to see this material

When I began working on this arrangement, I had an idea of the bass playing an exotic line and Jimmy playing the drums with his hands, sort of like a tabla. I'm not all that familiar with Indian music, so don't expect this to be authentic in any way. It's like going to an American restaurant and ordering a dish that is flavored with curry. I just had a vague idea of the kinds of exotica that Dennis and Jimmy could provide on bass and drums.

With that in the back of my mind, I sat at the piano and played through the song—first with the original rhythms, melody and harmonies, and then gradually re-harmonizing the melody to conform to the exotic world I had a picture of in my head. The idea was to retain as much of the original song as I could. I wanted to keep it simple on the head, so that the focus would be on the groove and the orchestration. As the chart went on, I could keep developing the material and get to wilder ideas.

The song itself is rather unusual, being nearly through-composed (very little material repeats verbatim), although the opening three-note descending motif and its counter-motif (built on the inversion of the motif in diminution) are the central ideas in all four 8-bar sections of the song *(Example 2-1)*.

Example 2-1

The harmonies are constantly changing underneath, so the only exact repetition occurs in bars 17–20. The form is *aba'c*. Here is the melody with the basic chord changes:

HINDUSTAN

Wallace/Weeks

I wrote the intro after I had completed the rest of the chart, so let's skip it for now, and start at letter **A**. The melody is in the flugelhorn (Trumpet 3) for the first 16 bars, and then switches over to Trumpet 1 for the next 16. The rhythm of the melody is pretty straight— much like the sheet music. No syncopations, very placid, which leaves me plenty of room for an active bass part. The melody consists primarily of minor 3rds and major 2nds, and is completely diatonic for 20 measures. Eventually we are introduced to the ♭7 (blue note) and then the ♭6 (which defines the *ivm*). That's it. I'm always amazed at songs that can evoke so much atmosphere while using so little chromaticism.

Honor and celebrate the climax

The climax of the melody (highest pitch) is the E at **D1**. We often like to draw attention to and celebrate the climax with a special chord. The high E reappears 5 bars later. It's usually not so good to repeat the highest pitch, but that's the melody we've all been playing for 100 years—it's a bit hard to change now. Fortunately, it goes by quickly. I gave it a bland harmonization on its second appearance, so as not to draw attention to the repetition and risk undermining the effect of the climax. The sudden wide intervals at the end of the song give a more daring character that is absent earlier.

Establish the melody/bass relationship

As I've said before (and I can't emphasize enough), the melody/bass relationship is of primary concern when determining the harmonies we want to use. Those two outside parts should sound complete by themselves. This is our meat and potatoes—everything else is gravy. The basic changes for this song are quite like *Tiger Rag*: 6 bars *I*, 8 bars *V*, 6 bars *I*, 2 bars *V/IV*, 2 bars *IV*. Then we have

the spot I love: 2 bars *V/V*, 2 bars *ivm*, 1 bar *ii*, 1 bar *V*, 2 bars *I*. Simple, right? Just play those roots against the melody, and it's already pretty good.

I don't need to dress it up too much. I'm going to add 6ths or major 7ths to the tonic chords and ♭7ths to the others (except for the *ivm* which will either get a 6th, a major 7th, or both). To relieve the monotony of 6 measures of the tonic at letter **A**, I used a passing dominant on beat 3 of **A2**. The melody note makes the 9th of the **G7**, so that is a somewhat sophisticated relationship.

Whole-tone scale Voicings

I've added a +5 to the G9. 9ths with +5's contain five of the six notes of the whole-tone scale. This kind of chord was popular in the 1920s and early '30s. It has a quaint sound— perfect for the character of this piece. Also note that the +5 of the dominant is the enharmonic equivalent of the ♭3 of the home key (a blue note). This gives us a slight tinge of the blues. I love the blues.

Expanding the Turnaround

At **A5** I use a *iii* chord to substitute for the *I*. This chord starts the journey to the dominant in **A7**. Rather than going directly to the dominant, I put the 5th in the bass, to create a bit of suspense. I could have made it a *ii* (Dm7), but I decided to save that for **B1** (2 bars later).

A6 presents an interesting situation. It starts out with a ♭*iii*⁰ (E♭⁰), which will move smoothly down by half step to the second inversion dominant (G7/D), except that the melody in the second half of the bar suggests C#⁰ (#*i*⁰), which then moves up to the G7/D. You'll notice that the bass has encircled this D with an upper neighbor and a lower neighbor. The E♭ to C# in the bass is a diminished 3rd, which is just a disguised (enharmonic) major 2nd. Since our melody is made up primarily of minor 3rds and major 2nds, this whole-step movement in the bass transforms the foreground (melody) into the background (bass movement). This is subtle, and maybe not noticeable to most listeners, but it affects us subliminally.

Using Sandwich Chords to Relieve Stasis

At **B2**, **B4**, **B5** and **B7** I used passing diminished chords to create good voice leading in all the parts. If the melody moved and the chord stayed the same, the under-parts would remain static. This lacks interest, and disengages those players that are not moving. Notice how those diminished chords resolve upwards. We had the same situation in *Stompin' On A Riff.*

B6 is a different situation. This measure will resolve to the tonic C in the next measure. If we work backwards (to paraphrase Oscar Hammerstein, a very good way to start), we can approach the C with a G7+5 (dominant approach). There is an A in the melody, creating the 9th on the G7+5. We had this chord earlier. Repeating chords, voicings, rhythms, etc. gives a piece of music character—especially if we are repeating an unusual sound. The G9+5 is preceded by a Dm7, which gives us a *ii V I* cadence. We often like to use the *ii* at the beginning of a *V* chord to give a suspension and resolution (4–3), while the bass moves down a 5th (or up a 4th). I have preceded the Dm7 with an Eb°. This is particularly nice because the melody makes the major 7th of the diminished. Not only that, but we have had a series of diminished chords that have resolved upwards, so this downward resolution satisfies our craving for up/down balance. The standard *I #i° ii V* turnaround works nicely in **B7-8**, since the melody note E makes the 3rd

of the first two chords, and then the 9th and 13th of the last two.

C1-4 is like **A1-4**, except that I use the G7+5 three times as a passing chord rather than just once, in order to accommodate a counterline in the bones and tenor. In **C5-6** I use the Gm to add a suspension/resolution to the C7. Rather than have the F of the Gm7 resolve down to the E of the C7, I chose to use a Gm (no 7th), move the 5th (D) up a half step to the +5 (D#) and ultimately up to the E (the 3rd of the C7).

I stayed with the original changes for **D1-4**, although when I go to orchestrate, I will add some pungent tensions to the voicings and thread a thumb line though them. In **D5**, rather than go directly to the *ii*, I postpone the *ii* for a measure and go to the *iii♭iii°* and then to our old friend *ii V I.*

Well, not so fast. The *iii* works particularly well, since the root is a half step below the root of the *ivm* in **D4**. The strongest root movement is down a 5th (up a 4th). The next strongest is chromatic movement (either ascending or descending by half step). The Eb° is nice because it reminds us of the Eb° to Dm7 from **B6**. When I resolve to the final tonic in **D7**, I just let the melody resolve, and keep everyone else on the dominant (G13–9). This creates an unexpected tension that is relieved on the downbeat of the next chorus.

[This treatment of the melody will be the basis for the entire arrangement, so I suggest that you listen again to the melody with the harmonic scheme, **2-4: (A-E)**. Does the music sound complete with just the melody and roots of the chords? If this is a good relationship, the inside parts of the chords should fill themselves in easily making good voice-leading.]

The Head

Voicing harmony notes above the melody

At **A** I chose to give the melody to the flugelhorn and keep it simple and square so that our attention will be drawn to the orchestration. I voiced out the melody in 4-part close harmony with one special touch. We have from top down C, B, G, E in the flugel, trombone, flute and tenor respectively. The special touch is that the flute part is up the octave, so he is a 5th above the flugel. The flugel has the melody, thereby giving the flute a harmony part above the melody.

This is a common technique in vocal writing, but a bit unusual (and therefore interesting) in instrumental writing. If the top voice is in a weak register on his instrument, and the melody is in a stronger register (or is a naturally louder instrument), we will get the desired blend, where the melody will prevail. In lieu of this, the top voice should play at a lower dynamic level. Notable examples of this texture can be found in Duke Ellington's music. One of my favorites is the first recording of *Drop Me Off In Harlem,* where the baritone sax has the melody in his mid-to-upper register, and three clarinets play close harmony above him in their weak break register.

Another interesting aspect of this first voicing is the half step between the flugel lead and the trombone. Normally a half step between the melody and a harmony note would create confusion for the listener—which is the lead? The trombonist, who is in his high register, must take care to not overpower the flugel in his middle register. The trombonist must also darken his sound (almost like a French horn) to blend with the flugel.

I didn't need to explain any of this to my players. They got the proper blend immediately, as they sight-read the chart. Honestly, I was a bit surprised that they could know all this, but they are not only great musicians, but very experienced at playing all kinds of music.

Doubling the Bass Part in the Bass Clarinets

The bass is given an active quasi-improvisational part that mostly arpeggiates the chords, in a melodic way, avoiding the notes of the flugel melody where possible. The two bass clarinets alternate doubling with the bass. The reason for using two bass clarinets instead of one is that there are no rests in the bass part. This is not a performance problem for the bassist, but bass clarinetists need rests in order to have time to breathe.

Linear Approach: Using a passing chord of like chord quality over a stagnant bass

Everything goes along smoothly until **A5** and **A6**, where the melody moves in quarter notes and the chords are stagnant. While the rhythm section plays Em7 for a bar, the horns play Dm9 Em9 Cmaj7 Em7. In the next bar the horns play Bb° Eb° F° C#°. Since the Bb° is over an Eb in the bass, it functions like an Eb7−9. Similarly the F° is over a C# in the bass and is a C#7-9. How did I arrive at these interesting chords? Actually they resulted from the individual lines moving parallel to the melody—linear writing. I don't inform the rhythm section of these passing chords. If the bass or piano were to catch them, they would interrupt the flow of their parts.

31

Altering Formula Voicings

Note that the flute sometimes switches from the third harmony part (transposed up the octave) to the second harmony part (up the octave). This is done to either make a better line for him, or to make better sounding voicings in the other parts. Letter **B** continues the same process for the first 6 bars.

[There is a lot to digest in this half-chorus. It would be a good idea to listen to these 16 bars 2-2: (A-C) before continuing. The tone of the entire piece is established here.]

Thumb lines foster continuity while creating subtle movement in static situations.

In **B7** the two remaining bones and the remaining tenor play a descending thumb line (cross-sectional orchestration), which continues for the first 4 bars of **C**, while the melody is transferred to the unison trumpets starting at **C**. This is the first time that there are no voicings, so we focus on the thumb line. Check out this thumb line. It starts on B, goes chromatically down to G and back up. Then it jumps up to D and goes chromatically up to E and back down. Interesting pattern, no?

Now look at how this line relates to the melody. The melody is diatonic and the thumb line is chromatic; also, the melody and thumb line are in contrary motion. These opposites are pretty cool—and will probably go unnoticed. What I like most about the thumb line is the blue notes—Bb's and Eb's. The melody is diatonic, but the blue notes make it feel like jazz.

The next 4 bars continue this idea but in a different orchestration. The 1st Trombone takes over the thumb line idea for 2 bars and then passes it over to the 2nd Trombone. While the 2nd Trombone is moving in half notes, the flugelhorn re-enters in chromatic quarter

notes. The tenor drops out in favor of voicings in the three bones for these 4 bars. I was very careful to avoid doubling pitches within the brass voicings. The only octave doublings are the momentary Bb and D quarter notes in **C5** and **6**.

The thumb line gets passed to the unison saxes on their sixteenth note pickups to letter **D**. I just noticed a very interesting *coincidence:* the chromatic sax pickup to **D** and next 2 bars have the same shape as the thumb line pickup and first 2 bars of **C**. The pitches are different and the rhythm of the pickup is different, but the shape is the same. The sax thumb line at **D**, however, continues downward for another 2 measures before it is passed off to the bones, who continue the thumb line for another bar. Letter **D** is 8 bars and has four different textures:

1. brass voicings with sax unison thumb line
2. trumpet unison melody with trombone thumb line
3. brass voicings with sax pedal
4. brass unison tonic with flugel/reed voicings alternating with the bass clarinet/bass.

Voicing the Brass

Let's look at the brass voicings. The 1st Trumpet has the melody. He starts on the 9th of the D7 (which is the secondary dominant *V/V*). Ever since I first heard *Take The "A" Train* over 50 years ago, I've been in love with the *V/V* and can't resist putting a +11 in it. Thank you, Mr. Strayhorn.

Jazz Lineage

Speaking of Billy Strayhorn... When I was a young man, I asked Bob Brookmeyer what his aesthetic was. He told me that he was just trying to sound like Gil (Evans). When I asked Gil the same question, he told me that he was just trying to sound like Billy Strayhorn. I once heard an interview with Count Basie, where he was asked a similar question. He responded that he wanted his band to sound like Duke Ellington's. When I told Jimmy Maxwell what Basie had said, Jimmy (who played with both Duke and Basie and was buddies with Basie) said with a smile, "Then I guess he was a terrible failure." The point of all of this is that we cannot help but be ourselves. As Oscar Wilde said:

"Be yourself. Everyone else is taken."

Back to the D7 or to be more complete, D13+11. 13th chords imply a natural 9th, unless otherwise stipulated. I voiced this D7 using an upper structure triad (E/D7). The trumpets play the E triad and the bones play a rootless D7. Upper structure triads give off a nice ring. Strangely enough, I don't move the voicing to accommodate the melody note D in **D2**. It seemed interesting to have the sax thumb line A♭ create the tritone with the D melody in the 1st Trumpet. Also, I like the unusual chord progression of D7 to Fm and didn't want to disturb it. Another nice relationship is that the 9th is doubled at the octave and then the top note resolves to the root, which, until that moment, is missing from the voicing—so we are satisfied to finally be grounded, even if the root is on the top of the voicing, rather than on the bottom.

The Fm not only has a major 7th but also a 6th and a 9th. Normally the 9th would not be unusual on a minor 7th chord, but it is rare to use it when the melody above it is on the 3rd (creating the very dissonant minor 9th interval). To make things even more starkly dissonant, the sax thumb line creates an *appoggiatura*

when it resolves the A♭/G dissonance to A♭/F. Thank you, Mr. Bach!

Advanced Voice Leading

Speaking of Bach, one of the "rules" we learned when writing Bach-style chorales was that the inside voices should not move from one note to another in a wider interval than the top voice moves, nor should one voice cross over another voice. The reasoning was that the inside part would be more interesting than the melody, and misdirect our attention away from the melody. It looks like I broke both of those rules going from the D7 to the Fm. Furthermore, the 3rd Trombone jumps down a minor 9th to the F. I'm sure there is a good reason why this works, but for now the only reason I can think of is:

Duke Ellington's rule: If it sounds good, it is good.

I like interesting inner parts. In fact if you play each part against each other part (two at a time), they all sound good. So much for rules—I'm going to stick with the Ellington rule. Sometimes I *like* to be distracted away from the melody with melodic inner parts.

Finishing the Head

There's nothing unusual in **D5**—just unison melody vs. unison thumb line. **D6** goes back to thick brass harmony. The Dm7 has the trumpets and flugel voiced in 3rds with the 1st and 2nd Trombone doubling the top two trumpets (down the octave) and Trombone 3 playing the 11th on the bottom. The resulting brass voicing is an Fmaj7 in the trumpets over a C triad in the bones. There is no root in the brass, so the saxes answer in unison a beat later with the missing D root and hold it over through the G7-9, which is also missing a D (the 5th) in the brass. The G7-9 is enriched by a 13th and a +11. This unstable chord creates a strong pull to resolve to the tonic. The melody in the three trumpets and two trombones holds out the C tonic while the flugel and saxes play tag with the unison bass clarinets and bass all on a G13-9 voiced with an upper structure E triad and finally resolve to a C69 on the *and* of beat 4 of **D8**.

[Listen to **2-3: (C-E)** for texture, counterpoint and voicings. Notice how all the horns float over the very active bass/bass clarinet line. They seem to exist in two different universes.]

Solos and Backgrounds

Solo #1 (over a choppy background): Establishing continuity during change

Normally in jazz we like to vary the bass lines and avoid repetition, in order to make the piece feel improvised and fresh. Conversely, in the 1930s, Duke Ellington would often use the same bass part for every chorus of an arrangement, or in some cases he would use it for just some of the choruses. This underlying repetition gave those pieces a feeling of unity that, because it was in the bass, most likely went unnoticed by listeners.

Following Ellington's lead, I devised a new bass line for the first two solo choruses (trombone and flugelhorn). I've also used the same chord changes for both choruses, so that when I change the orchestration, melody and voicings of the background figures, we still feel like we are in the same section of the piece.

Using the Bass and Drums to Define the Form

The new bass part for this section is the opposite of the previous chorus; syncopated roots and 5ths, rather than the stream of 8th notes. Another and more important difference is that the active bass line during the head was difficult to play and drew our attention. This new bass part presents no technical difficulty and lets the brass soloists have the spotlight all to themselves. Notice that Jimmy has added hi-hat on beats two and four of each bar. This not only adds to the groove, but also helps us to understand that that this is a new section.

Aside from keeping time, establishing the groove and adding color, the drummer is also responsible for delineating the form of the piece. He usually does this by changing cymbals, playing fills, or setting up new repetitive patterns.

Because the rhythm section has identical parts for both solo choruses, the brass only play their background on the first chorus, and the reeds only play on the second chorus, I was able to put a repeat around this 32-bar chorus and mark the parts accordingly. This shortens the parts, saving a page in some cases. In a fairly long chart like this one, having one less page to turn makes it easier on the performers.

Since the feeling is smooth and relaxed on the head, I shift gears for the first solo (trombone) and make the backgrounds choppy and agitated. On the second solo (flugelhorn) the backgrounds are smooth and soothing. The use of these opposites helps to keep the piece interesting and tell a story with varied episodes. Because the rhythm section is constant for these two choruses, there is plenty of continuity underlying these abrupt changes. The big surprises in this piece are to come later, when you don't expect them.

Some mute considerations

The brass background to the trombone solo defies Fletcher Henderson's "opposite choir" principle, but since the brass are playing short, choppy phrases and Ryan is playing

34

long legato solo lines in double time on trombone, there is no confusing the foreground and background. I thought about putting either the brass or solo trombone in mutes to differentiate their colors. Muting the brass section messes with the continuity more than I'd like to. I'm open to a mute on the trombone solo, so that might be a possibility for future performances. We have played this chart hundreds of times, and it never seemed like we needed to make a change, but I'd be open to it. One of the great things about jazz is, as Duke Ellington used to say about his music, it's in the process of becoming.

Some thoughts on accompaniment

When I write backgrounds for soloists (vocal as well as instrumental), I imagine the sound and style of the soloist and then think of what would make him/her sound good while transforming the motif or motifs from the head. Very often I use one technique per chorus or for an entire solo.

In this chart, the brass backgrounds for the trombone solo are all in the same register and, with the exception of one chord—at **H**, I use the same voicing technique: 4-part close harmony with a root added below. Although the voicings are creative, the spacings within them are similar. Notice that, although tensions are liberally applied (9ths, 11ths, 13ths and their alterations), each voice moves in a very natural, melodic way. Every voicing has five different pitches. The sameness in the brass helps us to keep our focus on the trombone solo.

Two unusual chords

I've introduced an interesting chord in **E6**: C#° over a D in the lowest trombone. The diminished upper part of the chord functions as

a leading tone diminished moving to a G7/D, while the D acts as the dominant of that upcoming G7. This chord gets repeated on the third beat of the next measure, and then many times throughout the rest of the arrangement.

Another interesting twist on the 4-part chord over a root happens on the Cmaj7/G in **F5**. Instead of a root (C) in the bottom trombone, I gave the 4th Trumpet the root and gave the 3rd Trombone the 9th. When I wrote the D on the bottom of the Cmaj7 voicing, my brain said, "Really? Why does that work?"

My first reaction was that it made a nice line for the 3rd Trombone, and it also related well to the resolution of the other notes above it and the bass line. One further thing has just occurred to me: it's the same D that has been on the bottom of the C#° voicings; a supertonic pedal point, if you will. This, along with the C#° with the D, makes two unusual voicings that I will exploit as the chart progresses.

Repeating an unusual sound or technique gives a piece character.

The chord at **H** is pretty standard: an upper-structure triad (E major) over the 3rd and 7th of a secondary dominant (D7); in this case a *V/V*. This is the climax of the song. Also, D7 is the most interesting chord in the progression. Changing the voicing reinforces its importance.

In **H4-6** the 3rd Trombone plays independent dominant pedal backbeats along with Jimmy's hi-hat leading into the final cadence with the 9th on the bottom of the Cmaj7 voicing.

[Let's listen to this chorus **2-5: (E-I 1st X)** with four things in mind:

1. How do the bass/brass and bone fit together?

2. How do the brass voicings sound?

3. See if you can listen to the individual brass parts and follow one voice at a time.

4. When playing arrangements with unusual voicings, it is critical that the players be balanced, in tune with centered tones, and play with absolute assurance. We are all trained as musicians to match the player next to us, so that we are in pitch, time and dynamics—all with the same concept, sounding as one.

Contrapuntal music is difficult because it challenges the players to do the opposite; play differently from the others—like when we were kids and sang *Row, Row Your Boat* in a round, and you had to stick your fingers in your ears, so the other kids wouldn't throw you off.

Dissonance and counterpoint will sound like mistakes if not played with utter confidence by all concerned. This takes musicians of high caliber, who believe that the arranger knows what he is doing.

Trombonist Al Cobbs once told me a funny story about playing with the Ellington band for the first time. He sat down next to Britt Woodman. Britt, who hardly ever spoke about how to play, turned to Al and said, "Trust your part. You're gonna see an F# and think that it should be an F natural. Play the F#. After a while you will come to love it."

My music looks fairly simple on the page, but when you actually play your part in the context of the entire band playing theirs, you are constantly challenged by the other musicians playing pitches and rhythms so contrary to yours. The result is that you question if you are correct. I am eternally grateful to all the cats in my band for their excellent musicianship, their belief in me, and

their conscientiousness to play this difficult music on such a high level.]

Solo #2 (over a smooth background)

Let's move on to the flugelhorn solo. The 5-reed background at **E** has the unusual instrumentation of flute, clarinet, tenor sax and two bass clarinets. This choice of instruments has as much to do with the sound I wanted, as it does with the instruments available.

Practicality can inspire creativity.

When I was about to write this chart, my second alto player, Matt Hong, told me that he had just gotten a new bass clarinet and would love to play it in the band. Until then, all the bass clarinet parts were written on the 5th Reed part, which is standard for most bands. Although the guys in my sax section all play a pile of doubles, they only have two hands each, which means I have to limit my writing to what they can carry to gigs. Since Matt had volunteered to bring his bass clarinet in addition to his alto sax, flute and clarinet, how could I pass up this opportunity?

When Jay and Dan saw Matt's bass clarinet, they informed me that they too could bring theirs. This prompted me to write an arrangement of *Last Night When We Were Young* for Jon Hendricks to sing with us, featuring four bass clarinets. What a sound! But that's another story.

For **Hindustan** I wanted flute on the top part. Jay is a fine flute player and would play his part with the sensitivity it cries out for. Dan is a virtuoso clarinetist, so that too is a no-brainer. Mark is the master of playing the tenor sax extremely softly and, by using sub-tone, able to blend with any instrument. Carl is our usual bass clarinetist. He studied with Joe Temperley; 'nuff said. The recording of

Hindustan was made while we were on tour in Sweden. Matt was unable to make that tour, but fortunately, our ace sub Todd Bashore was available. Todd doesn't play bass clarinet, so he took over Jay's flute part while Jay played Matt's bass clarinet part on the recording. One thing jazz teaches us is flexibility.

Consistency

So now, the challenge is how to get these disparate reed instruments to blend into a choir. I kept the flute in his low register. He never goes above an E in the staff. That will give this section a soft, gauzy sound. (Note that for the flute to be heard when playing in this register, the rest of the band must be soft and the drummer must keep off the cymbals).

The reeds start with two notes in octave unison before spreading out into a Drop 2 voicing with an added root below. I mostly continue to use this spacing with a few little twists (like putting the ♭2 on the bottom of diminished chords or the 5th or the 9th on the bottom of the tonic).

At **F5** the reeds go into 4-part close harmony with a root (♭2 or 9th) on the bottom, just as the brass had done in the previous chorus. On the third beat of **F8** the tenor is on the ♭5 of the G7 and the clarinet (the next voice up) is on the 7th. This left a nice opportunity to fill in the interval with 8th notes and give the line a bit of motion to cover up the seam between letters **F** and **G**. This is reminiscent of the 16th note pickup into **D**, but twice as slow. The first 2 bars at **G** repeat the first 2 bars of **E** for continuity. Then it's back to 4-part close over the root (or its odd substitutes), until **G7** where the *IV* chord suggests a new approach.

The rhythm section and soloist stay on the F chord for 2 bars, while the reeds move through

a series of passing chords: Fmaj9 Gm9 G#°/C Am9 B♭69 Bm11-5 Fmaj9 (with the tenor moving −5, ♮5, +5, 6).

At **H** we are back to the long/short note pattern with D13+11 resolving down to an A♭9-5 and then Fm(maj7)/G to Fm6/G (the last chord is repeated for final punctuation). Notice how the reeds at **H** play descending syncopations (a development of **G5**) as opposed to the ascending half notes and whole notes at **E**, **F** and the first 2 bars of **G**. These opposites give us a feeling of completeness. Just to leave the door open, I let the reeds rest for the last 4 bars before the end of the chorus, so the flugelhorn soloist can get the last word in the clear, and cleanse our palates for the bass clarinet duet at **I**.

[At this point I recommend listening to this chorus a second time, **2-6: (E-I 2nd X)**—flugel solo with reed backgrounds) paying particular attention to:

1. The sonority of the blended reeds.
2. The voice leading.
3. How smoothly the passing chords move.
4. How each chorus of this chart develops in its own way, but that we never lose the overall feeling of the piece.]

Solo #3 (an improvised duet)

The bass clarinet duet chorus (**I** through **L**) presents several orchestration problems:

1. Bass clarinets are soft. The accompaniment must be softer.
2. Much of the bass clarinet's range is in the same range as that of the bassist.
3. How do we organize the two soloists so that they will complement each other?

I love the sound of the bass clarinet, but I often hear jazz musicians overblow it, thereby getting a harsh sound. I don't think they *want* to overblow, but because the rhythm section is so loud and busy, they feel the need to play as loud as possible to be heard. To prevent this from occurring, I have the piano *tacet* and have the drummer play softly on the rims of the snare.

Leaving Space

Since the bass and bass clarinet share the same basic range and function, I have the bass play sparsely—leaving plenty of space for the bass clarinets to have a dialogue. It is also essential that the bass not be amplified. Once we played the chart, I encouraged Dennis to feel free to play what he wanted on this chorus, as long as it remained sparse and defined the chord progression.

When we first rehearsed this chart, I told the bass clarinetists that one should play mostly in the lower register, and the other mostly in the high register. By doing so, they would ensure that the listener could follow each player and not get confused.

Backgrounds

The first and third 8-bar sections of this chorus have only sparse bass and rims for background behind the soloists. The second and fourth 8-bar sections have only a few sustained chords. The brass is in cup mutes and the remaining three reeds (flute, clarinet and tenor) are mixed in for color. The cup mutes soften the brass and take off much of their high frequencies, so that they don't compete with the bass clarinet soloists for attention.

The few passing chords at **J** use the diminished with the ♭9 on the bottom. In this case they are F♯° chords. The G on the bottom is the dominant in the key of C (dominant pedal point). The next voice above him (2nd Trombone)

repeats C's (tonic pedal point). He holds onto his C, even when the harmony moves to G7.

Pedal points have a way of obscuring the harmony somewhat, without losing our ears' relationship to the tonic. The dominant pedal point in the bass for the last 2 bars of this chorus creates tension that wants to resolve on the succeeding downbeat.

The final 2 bars of this chorus (**L7-8**) have a pyramid in the suddenly straight muted brass. Straight mutes retain the highs of open brass, but at a much lower volume. They also have a slightly pinched tone.

At this point in the song we arrive at the tonic (C chord) played in this order: 1, 9, 5, 3, 6, maj7, and +11. Although the pyramid basically ascends, the third trombone note (played by Trombone 2) and the fourth trumpet note (played by flugelhorn) are lower than the previous pitches. In addition, the jerky 8th note rhythmic pattern (3+3+4+6) feels a bit off-kilter. Also note that the bass and drums are encouraged to crescendo to help set up the shout chorus, which begins on the downbeat of the next bar (**M1**).

[Let's listen to **2-7: Bass Cl Soli (I-M)**. Note how the colors and textures have changed from the previous chorus. Everything is thinned out. This is the calm before the storm.]

The Shout Chorus (where everything comes together)

Although this chorus doesn't really shout (as in a swing chart), it serves as the climax of the piece. This is where we transform the ideas that have been developing and take them to their extremes. I'm looking for the band to go wild, and yet I need to keep continuity with what has come before. Like Hamlet, there's a method to my madness. This chorus is the ultimate challenge for me. It should sound crazy, but somehow logical.

*Remember that in music we are telling a **story**. The audience must be willing and able to follow us.*

Train Onomatopoeia

From letter **M** through **P**, I am trying to give the effect of an Indian railroad train. Train onomatopoeia is prevalent throughout the blues and jazz, but almost always, those are the sounds of American trains. I highly recommend listening to the following Ellington train pieces:

> *Daybreak Express*
> *Happy-Go-Lucky Local*
> *Track 360*
> *The Old Circus Train Turn-around Blues*
> *Loco Madi*

And of course, the 1941 Ellington recording of Billy Strayhorn's *Take The "A" Train.*

I also recommend Wynton Marsalis' *Big Train,* which was recorded by the Jazz at Lincoln Center Orchestra.

I've seen a number of movies that take place in India, that include train rides. Most if not all of these movies take place a long time ago. The trains are rickety and seriously overcrowded.

Commuter train in Mumbai. Courtesy of www.India.com.

I wanted to capture the rickety rhythm of the wheels and carriages, the speed and power of the locomotive, and the shrill train whistle. Now, the question is how to accomplish all this, using the motifs that have already been introduced.

Keep in mind that after the exposition (in this case, the first chorus), it is best not to introduce new motives. This confuses the listener and makes the piece superficial. What we really want in the shout chorus is to hear the transformation of the existing material, so that it:

1. comes to a satisfying climax.

2. shows us how the original motif and its opposite are at the same time, opposites and the same.

At **M** Trumpets 1, 2 and 4, the three trombones doubled two octaves below (for an exotic effect), the arco bass doubled an octave below the trombones and the piano two octaves above the trumpets as well as in the low octave with the bass represent the power and speed of the train. The brass glide over the churning rhythm of the reeds, flugelhorn and drums.

Making adjustments on the fly

Originally I had the brass open, but as soon as I heard this section when we sight-read the chart, I realized that open brass were covering up all the interesting delicate material in the reeds. I switched the brass to straight mutes, which keep the brightness and intensity of the brass sound, but at a much lower volume and a bit pinched in tone color, which is perfect for the Asian sound. The pitches (E, G, A, B) are the same notes as the quarter notes played by the flugelhorn starting on the third beat of **A4**. These four notes are the retrograde of the first four notes in the flugel at **A**, if you make the first note at **A** a half-step lower (which is the pitch Trombone 1 is playing).

I've altered the rhythm of this motif to equal-value half notes. **M3** uses diminution—the same four notes played twice as fast (quarter notes). Although I've decided to retain the foursquare harmonic rhythm as underpinning, I upset the symmetry by giving the drums a 2-bar solo in **A4** and **5**. **M1** and **2** come back in **M6** and **7**, followed by another 2-bar drum solo, which goes past letter **N** by one bar.

The half note motif is repeated in **N2** and **3**, but the first two notes are altered (the first is up a half step, while the second is down a half step), so that they are chromatic, not unlike the melody in **D4** (only a major 2nd below). This 2-bar half note phrase is followed by a 1-bar drum solo, which sets up the brass squarely on the symmetrical 5th bar of **N** for their quarter note repetition of the motif. Next, we hear a 3-bar drum solo, which completes the first half of the chorus and plants us firmly on the downbeat of letter **O**.

Notice how I only used one idea in half the band—the 4-note motif. Through diminution and metrical displacement, it gives the illusion of being organic, but at the same time lopsided. This entire chorus owes much to the music of Igor Stravinsky. I love the logic of his construction and his complex textures built out of several simple ideas in counterpoint. I spent two years studying *The Rite Of Spring*, in addition to a lifetime of enjoying many of his other pieces. *The Rite Of Spring* is now 100 years old, and is still the most modern piece of music I know.

6-Part Counterpoint

Let's look at what the reeds and flugelhorn are doing at **M** and **N**. I've included the flu-gel with the reeds as a substitute for a French horn. We don't have a horn in our band, so the flugel is the closest I can get to a brass instrument that will blend in a similar way with the woodwinds. Here is how this section breaks down:

- Flute pairs with clarinet—8th notes in contrary motion—major 2nds alternating with major 7ths.

- Flugelhorn pairs with bass clarinet—quarter notes in contrary motion—major 9ths alternating with minor 2nds.

- Bass clarinet performs the bass line 3/8 pattern.

- Tenor sax, the wild card playing the retrograde of the brass motif, boldly moves against the entire ensemble in quarter note triplets.

Notice the similarity of the two pairs and how they move at different speeds. I made chromatic adjustments to fit the harmonies of the song, while the brass pretty much ignore the changes. The reeds and brass have distinctly different characters, since they represent different sounds of the train, but nonetheless in gear and moving forward.

Shifting Gears for the Brass/Reed Dogfight

Letter **O** is a series of 1-bar exchanges with the drums: brass, drums, reeds, drums, bones, drums, piano/bass, drums. There is a need to build intensity, so I switch gears into a double time feel and have the brass remove their mutes. Following the previous pattern of the six reeds in **M** and **N** (I'm treating the flugel as a member of the reed section), the six brass play wild counterpoint, also using some pairs:

- Trumpets 1 and 2 play a syncopated figure in contrary motion, using the same notes as the flute and clarinet did at **O**.

- Trumpet 4 and Trombone 2 each play 16 sixteenth notes, but with very different shapes.

- Trumpet 4 has four groups of sixteenths—each starting on the beat.

- Trombone 2 plays the 3/8 pattern. There is some contrary motion and a variety of intervals—most notably major 7ths.

- Trombone 3 plays a bass pattern.

- Trombone 1 is the wild card, utilizing the characteristic sounds of the trombone—sliding up to the note and then employing wild slide vibrato.

In **O3** the reeds answer in pairs:

- Flute and flugelhorn have sixteenth notes in contrary motion.

- The bass clarinets have a bass line split between them.

- Tenor sax has chromatic eighth notes ascending and descending.

- Clarinet is the wild card, with sixteenth note sextuplets.

The trombones in **O5** reverse the reed pattern:

- The top two bones play eighth notes in contrary motion alternating minor 2nds and major 7ths.

- Trombone 3 is the wild card, with the chromatic ascending/descending figure—this time in 16th notes.

When it came time for the piano/bass statement in **O7**, I decided to leave it up to them to create something interesting. By now they have heard three horn statements and three drum answers. They will know what to do.

The drum solo in **O8** transitions back to single time (from double time feel) and also makes a

crescendo to set up the four loud train whistle toots in **P1-3**. These are very loud and percussive as well as being the most dissonant and dense chords in the entire chart. Notice the use of minor 9th intervals—flute/Trumpet 2 (the 5th on top of +11), Trumpet 4/Trombone 2 (9 on top of -9) in **P1-2**. **P3** is basically an Fm chord with a 6, major 7, 11 and +11. These are highly dissonant chords. I reserve this sort of thing for special effects—in this case train whistles.

Transition to the Recapitulation

The diminuendo in **P4** sets up the piano and bass, who answer the horns (as they did in **O7**). This time there are 2 bars concerted and then 2 bars of piano solo over bass setting up the return of the bass figure at **A**. The chord progression in **P5-6** is basically | Em7 Eb° | Dm7 Db7 | which then resolves to the tonic C major. I chose not to use a turnaround to return to letter **A**. After all the craziness in this chorus, it feels so nice to relax for 2 bars on the tonic.

As for the chromatic chords in **P5-6**, the piano right hand plays mainly diminished structures, while his left hand stays on pedals that rub. The bass moves down chromatically using double stops in 5ths. These chords create a high degree of tension at a lower volume than the horns, before melting into the much-needed resolution in **P7**.

[Let's listen to **2-8: Shout Chorus (M-D.S al Coda)**. Does it develop the motifs to a satisfactory climax (**P3**)? For all the fancy writing, it's really a chorus of drum exchanges. My intent was for this chorus to be wild in direct contrast to the recap of the melody, which is oh, so sedate.]

Recapitulation and Coda

All that is left now is to *DS* back to **A** and play the first 30 bars of the head, 2 bars drums and then a 4-bar vamp for both bass clarinets, which is followed by an ensemble ♭*VII7* chord in the ensemble, while the bass clarinets continue to solo over the fermata. The ♭*VII7* chord (B♭9+11) works so well because the upper structure triad (C major) is the tonic chord, but the B♭7 underneath it disrupts the tonality.

Introduction

Now I had material to draw on for the intro. I lifted the reed/flugelhorn texture from let-ter **M** for 3 bars, followed by 2 bars of drums (upsetting the symmetry), 2 bars of piano solo, and finally a bar of drums to set up the head. By using this material from the shout chorus, I set up the mood of the piece and at the same time prepare the shout chorus, so that when we get there it feels not only natural, but inevitable.

[Let's listen again to the entire chart, **2-1: Complete Arrangement**. This is an unusual piece for me in many ways. I had a lot of fun writing it as well as performing it a couple of hundred times. Our band always feels challenged and inspired to invent things we didn't even know we had in us.]

3. Do It Again

[At www.suchsweetthundermusic.com/pages/
cjca-accompanying-files listen to **3-1: Complete Arrangement**. Now ask yourself these
three questions that I ask myself whenever I
listen to music:

1. What do you like about this chart?
2. What don't you like?
3. How might you do it differently?]

This early song composed by George Gershwin with lyrics by Buddy DeSylva is a model
of simplicity. Gershwin gets so much mileage

George Gershwin in 1935

out of the descending
major scale. The form
of the song is *abab'*.
The *b'* section consists
of 4 bars repeating the
original *b*, but instead
of ending on a semi-
cadence, as in the first
b section, it moves to a
full cadence.

The words and melody fit so well together. "Oh, do it again" falls off the tongue in a
perfect colloquial manner on the descending scale, and then the song follows its own
lyric demand and does it again. (Of course
DeSylva's lyric is referring to kissing, and the
double entendre makes it even better.) George
Gershwin wrote the music when he was about
20 years old. Even at that young age, he understood songwriting on the deepest level.

Getting Started

I like arranging 32-bar song forms. It's a challenge to be creative and not repeat myself. I
started working on this chart in the same manner that I do most arrangements of songs—by
playing the song over and over on the piano,
finding the harmonies that best convey the
spirit and character of the particular song and
restating the rhythms of the melody so that
they feel conversational and swinging. Once I
feel comfortable, it's time to take out the score
paper and pencil.

I normally start arranging at letter **A** (where
the song begins) and then write the intro when
I know what the piece is about. We saw that
procedure in *Hindustan*. Sometimes I begin
by writing the intro. In many cases I wind up
either rewriting the intro or throwing it out
altogether, but every once in a while I seem to
get it right. **Do It Again** is one of those times
when I could see where the piece was going
before I even scored the head—well, almost.

When we sight-read this chart in rehearsal, I
decided to add a chorus of piano solo before
the intro, as was the custom in such great
bands as Count Basie, Duke Ellington and
Thad Jones/Mel Lewis. In this case the written
intro sounds better after the piano solo than
without it. However, the arrangement could
work either way.

The Intro

Although Gershwin's central motif is a 5-note
descending major scale starting on the 3rd
and descending to the 6th, I decided to start
the intro with a 3-note segment of the scale in
the unison saxes (the 2nd down to the 7th) and
gradually expand it, so that we don't hear the
full five notes until letter **A**. The intro should
be a tease—you don't want to give away too
much.

*Differentiate opposing contrapuntal ideas
rhythmically, melodically, and in many cases
orchestrationally and texturally.*

The brass and rhythm section answer with a 2-note syncopated rhythmic figure (a displaced Charleston rhythm—it starts on the third beat rather than the first beat of the bar). While the saxes hold out the major 7th of the tonic F chord in unison, the brass play repeated F69 chords. Keeping the sax note out of the brass voicings gives each section a different character.

The next 2 bars are quite similar. The rhythms and textures are identical, but the saxes invert their line (tonic moving diatonically up to the 3rd) and the brass play a ♭VII7 chord (E♭13) while the saxes hold out their A which is the +11 of the E♭7. Although the sax line is diatonic, the landing notes (E and A) become interesting notes in the harmonies. I wrote the melody first and then chose harmonies that would make those melody notes sound interesting.

Notice that I don't use all the instruments in the band. The 2nd Alto and 2nd Trumpet are omitted because they will be featured throughout the entire arrangement, as soloists and as a small group within the big band. I'll save the alto sax/trumpet color until letter **A**, so that the orchestration will help the listener to understand the form.

The bari rests during these sax unisons because I'm looking for a lighter sound, and the bari would add too much weight at the unison, either in his extreme high register or an octave below. I save his entrance for when the saxes go into harmony in the fifth bar. Similarly, the piano doesn't come in until the pick-up to **A**, where we go into a two-beat feel.

Here's an advanced concept: Unisons within voicings can work if they move to the next note by contrary motion. Sometimes it's possible to arrive at the unison in contrary motion as well.

I did something a bit unusual in the brass voicings. The F69 voicing has only five different pitches, and I've got six available brass, so I doubled the top two trumpets. I don't normally like to double the top note of a voicing. In fact I generally try to avoid doubling within sections (and with the exception of *tutti* voicings, I try to give each horn its own pitch). When two parts double a pitch, I will have them move in contrary motion to the following pitch, which is exactly what happens with Trumpets 1 and 3.

With the exception of completely parallel voicings, this same principle regarding contrary motion applies to octave doublings in non-*tutti* passages. I rarely double the bottom trumpet and the top trombone, but that also can be nice if it involves contrary motion.

Sometimes it is effective to begin a phrase in unison, and at the appropriate, logical moment, switch to voicing the line. The reverse can work as well.

The saxes start the next phrase exactly like their first phrase, but on the third note they go into harmony while they pass the melodic ball to the unison brass, who play chromatic alterations of the inverted motif. The bari enters on the 11th of the Am7, creating a voicing with intervals of a 3rd on top and 4ths below.

There is no root in the horns. It is quickly supplied by the brass on the *and* of beat 1 and the bass on beat 2. Similarly, the bari has the 5th on the bottom of the D7+9 with the bass finally sounding the root on beat 4. The Gm7 voicing in the saxes on beat 4 *and* has the 11th on top rather than the 5th. For this brief moment, the brass and saxes come to agreement on C (the dominant of our key of F). The reason this sounds strong to me is the contrary motion (alto sax descending a 4th and brass ascending by whole step.

Constant structure chords can relieve the predictability of our normal tonal harmonies.

The harmonized saxes then answer with four syncopated quarter notes descending in whole steps (a whole-tone variation of the four-note descending motif) in constant structure major 7th chords voiced in open position. The unusual chromatically altered B♮ in the lead alto on the first syncopated chord can sound striking at first, but is quickly justified when we realize that it is part of a pattern of constant structure chords. This is so interesting that it will need to be developed later in the chart.

Very often the rhythm section can smooth out the seams between adjacent sections of the piece.

As the saxes hold out the last chord, the rhythm section (with the piano finally added) sets up the 2-beat feel for the melody chorus at letter **A**. As you can see (and hear), you can get a lot of mileage out of brass versus saxes just by changing textures. Many arrangers tend to want to harmonize everything. Not utilizing a variety of textures is as limiting as playing everything at the same volume (which, unfortunately, many bands do nowadays).

The Head

At letter **A** we expect two things:

1. The melody of the song.
2. A steady groove (could either be in two or four). Traditionally, dance bands of the swing era played the melody chorus in two, and then would shift gears into four for the solos and shout chorus.

I feel a need to deliver on both expectations, but not without some surprises. I've been resting the 2nd Alto and 2nd Trumpet, so that when they come in with the melody in unison at **A**, they will create a fresh color. These

two instruments remain coupled in unison for much of the piece and are also featured as the soloists. This new color (trumpet/alto sax unison) or "section" can be added to our arsenal of sax section, brass section and trombone section.

Thoughts on the Trumpet Section

Note that the trumpets are not used as an independent section until the fifth bar of **B**. Many arrangers don't use the harmonized trumpet section without the trombones supporting them underneath. They have no problem with unison trumpets alone. I used to feel this way many years ago.

When I was young, I was very influenced by Thad Jones. He rarely used harmonized trumpets alone. Mostly he would put the trombones below them, or the bones and the saxes. In *'A That's Freedom* he has the saxes below the trumpets while the bones play a unison counter-line. I do all these things as well, but I'm also comfortable with the trumpets by themselves for a pure color. They can be middle to low register or upper register.

Actually, one of Thad's signature moments comes in the second to last bar of *Big Dipper*, where the four trumpets play Ellington's *Band Call* in their upper register. The top three trumpets are in parallel first inversion triads, while the 4th Trumpet is in major 7ths below the lead trumpet. This is a truly spectacular ending, maybe in part because we almost never hear the trumpets by themselves in Thad's music, so the brightness grabs us.

Another one of my favorite moments in Thad's charts is the intro to *Woman's Got Soul* from the album ***Presenting Joe Williams and Thad Jones Mel Lewis–The Jazz Orchestra***. If you don't know this record, I encourage you to listen to it. It may be the greatest vocal album ever made. The charts are nothing short of wonderful, as is Joe's singing and the band's playing. *Woman's Got Soul* begins with *a cappella* four trumpets in their low register harmonized in simple 4-part harmony (another rarity in Thad's writing).

You'll notice that, although I use the complete range of the trumpets in my writing, I save the upper register for when I *really* need power and brightness. Too much high trumpet can become irritating and also lose its shock value. A little bit goes a long way. Having come up playing in trumpet sections, I am very sensitive to where the trumpets sound best and contribute the most to an arrangement.

Choose your keys and registers wisely.

Many years ago I wrote a pile of arrangements for The Duke's Men, which started out as a cooperative group of Ellington alumni. After a short while, trombonist Art Baron became the leader and paid me a nice compliment, which has stayed with me. He said that in my charts every instrument is always in the exact right place on his horn to make the figures and lines sound right for the message they need to convey. In many arrangers' work, the horn players struggle to make their parts sound appropriate, and blend. Very often you feel that your part should be a 4th or 5th above or below where you are written.

As a young man, I once saw Sy Oliver's small band play at the Rainbow Room. I asked him why he was playing his hit charts from the Jimmie Lunceford band in different keys from the famous recordings. He told me that, with less brass, he needed to lower the keys. This makes perfect sense—you don't want the trumpet up high with no support—and be-

sides, by that time Sy didn't have a lot of high chops.

Write what sounds good for the musicians who will be playing.

When choosing the key to write an arrangement, the arranger most often uses the key of the sheet music, or the original jazz recording. You don't have to. I often do this, but I don't feel any special allegiance to those keys. I choose the key that puts all the instruments in their best registers to express the figures I have in mind. Vocal charts are a similar, but slightly different story. Since the singer is the focus of any vocal arrangement, you must find the key that works best for him or her, then write figures for the band that work in that key. (I'll deal with vocal charts specifically in *Volume II* of this series.)

The other surprise at letter **A** is that the two-beat feel starting at **A** is delayed by two beats because of the hit on the *and* of beat 1 in the first bar of **A**. The brass play a Gm7-5 built up in 3rds with the 11th on the top and bottom. Everyone is in a bright, strong area of his instrument for this rhythmic jab. I usually like to put some dissonance in rhythmic hits to add to the percussive effect. In this chord, the D♭ rubs against both the C above it and the C below it, and the B♭ rubs against the A in the alto/trumpet unison.

Back to Basics

Before we go any further, let's take a look at the original lead sheet of this 92-year-old song. The chord changes are simple, but they relate to the melody in an interesting way that beckons me to dress them up a bit, so as to give them more of the character I see peeking out at me.

DO IT AGAIN

Words by Buddy Desylva
Music by George Gershwin

Example 3-1. Original sheet music.

This is how this song appeared in the original sheet music *(Example 3-1)*. George Gershwin supplied the melody, and Buddy DeSylva wrote the words. We can't be sure about the harmonies. In many cases in sheet music, the composer wrote basic chord changes and an arranger, who was hired by the publisher, wrote the piano arrangement and added his own harmonies. If we take away the adornments, the basic harmonies of this song look like this (Example 3-2):

I like some of the added harmonies from the sheet music and will incorporate them into my chart. I feel no obligation to use or not use any of them. I feel the same way about the rhythms. I generally find the rhythms in sheet music to be stiff and not the way we speak. Although there is some syncopation in the sheet music of this song, I'm going to add a little more. I don't change the pitches of the

DO IT AGAIN

Words by Buddy Desylva
Music by George Gershwin

Example 3-2. Original sheet music, basic harmonies.

original melody or mess with the words. After all, that is what the song is all about and what drew me to it.

Authorship

When Bob Brookmeyer returned from California in 1978, he started pushing the compositional envelope even further than he had before leaving New York seven years earlier. Shortly after his return, he started teaching. He said that, traditionally, arrangers dress up their baby in different clothes, but what he was interested in doing was dismantling the baby and putting the head back where the arm used to be, etc.

When Bob and I worked together with Gerry Mulligan's Concert Jazz Band, one of my favorite arrangements was Bob's version of *My Funny Valentine*. Later on in 1979 or 1980, Bob wrote a new arrangement of the same song for Mel Lewis's band (which had been the Thad Jones/Mel Lewis Jazz Orchestra and still exists as the Vanguard Jazz Orchestra).

This new arrangement of *My Funny Valentine* bears little resemblance to the Rodgers and Hart standard. Bob had dismembered it and reassembled an abstract piece, so that even Dick Rodgers and Larry Hart would never in a million years recognize their song. I understand that Bob had begun with the Rodgers and Hart song and was inspired by it—but why should two deceased songwriters' estates collect the royalties when this is clearly a new work?

What if you are driving your car and it starts to rain? You turn on the windshield wipers. Suddenly the rhythms of the rain hitting the windshield and the steady beat of the wipers inspire you to create a piece of music. Should you credit the rain and the wipers? Or, as in the case of Ellington and Strayhorn's *Blue-bird Of Delhi* from the *Far East Suite*, should the bird on Duke's windowsill be regarded as the composer? After all, Duke heard his song and whistled it to Strays on the phone. Did Ellington or Strayhorn make any changes? Certainly Strayhorn added harmony and the arrangement. How close to the bird's song is the final product? Do we care?

The question of authorship is a sticky one. Ellington was often accused of "stealing" songs from his sidemen. It is true that he paid Cootie Williams $75 for the first 2 bars of *Concerto For Cootie* (which later became *Do Nothing Till You Hear From Me*). He also paid Johnny Hodges $75 for his warmup lick (the first 2 bars of *Never No Lament*, which became *Don't Get Around Much Anymore*). Neither Johnny nor Cootie had any intention of creating a song from their licks, but Duke heard a song and developed it. At least Johnny and Cootie got the $75 they had agreed to. In 2014, that $75 would be worth $1248.47. If you want to pay me $1248.47 for a two-measure lick, I'll be happy to sell it to you! You can do anything you want with it. How many would you like?

Cootie once told me that the first 3 bars of *Stormy Weather* were something that he used to play at the Cotton Club. Harold Arlen heard it, and put it in the Cotton Club show they were rehearsing at the time. As Cootie said to me, "The man stole my music and made a million dollars." Then again, a decade later, Cootie convinced a young and largely unknown pianist who was composing tunes for Cootie's big band, to put Cootie's name as co-composer on *'Round Midnight*. What goes around comes around.

The point of all this is: inspiration comes from many places. When appropriate, it is ethical to give credit where credit is due. We all use

DO IT AGAIN

Words by Buddy Desylva
Music by George Gershwin

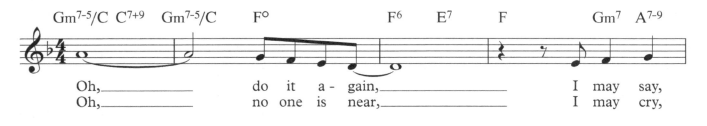

Oh,_____ do it a - gain,_____ I may say,
Oh,_____ no one is near,_____ I may cry,

"no, no, no, no, no," but do it a-gain.___ My lips just
"oh, oh, oh, oh, oh," but no one will hear.___ Ma - ma may

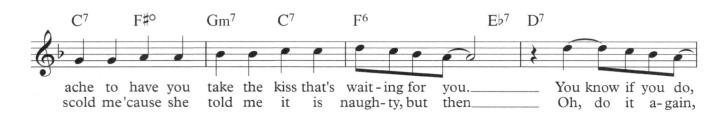

ache to have you take the kiss that's wait-ing for you.___ You know if you do,
scold me 'cause she told me it is naugh-ty, but then___ Oh, do it a-gain,

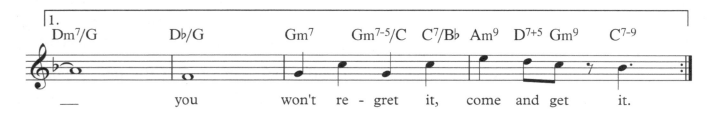

_ you won't re - gret it, come and get it.

Please do it a - gain!

Example 3-3.

phrases that we have heard in other people's music, but when we organize them in a new way, they can become our composition. If we still hear the source(s) as relating to someone else's work, then it is only fair to credit them and use their title.

Here is a lead sheet with the alterations I used for the first chorus of this arrangement (**Example 3-3**). Notice how few changes I made from the original sheet music—and how most of those changes are pretty subtle. I've kept the melody intact with the exception of deleting the melody in measure 30. Sometimes in personalizing a melody we add notes, and sometimes we subtract notes while keeping the form. In this arrangement I also elided the last 2 bars of the song form (making it only 30 measures long) and then re-used the intro as an interlude.

Intros, Interludes and Codas

Since intros are made up of the essential DNA of the piece, they often work as codas. When this happens (as it often does, particularly in small group arrangements), they are sometimes called *outros*. In this arrangement the intro works nicely as an interlude between the melody chorus and the alto solo.

Interludes should be of a different character from the melody, so that it is clear that we are not in the song form. The same is true of intros.

When codas are extensions of the melody, we normally call them *tags* or *tag endings*. In many cases I think of interludes as intros to the next section of the piece.

A classic piece that re-uses the interlude is Neal Hefti's *Flight Of The Foo Birds*, which was recorded by Count Basie. The interlude first comes between the melody chorus and the first solo chorus, and then reappears after the last solo and introduces the shout chorus. I love how interludes say to the listener, "Something new and important is about to happen."

Dominant Substitution

Rather than sit on a chord for a series of notes, I often like to use dominant approach chords to create better voice leading and to give the feeling of motion. In the case of this song, the first 4 bars are essentially the tonic. Rather than alternate tonics and dominants, I treated

the first six beats as the dominant, then moved to a tonic diminished before resolving to a tonic 6th chord. The Gm7-5/C chords serve merely as appoggiaturas to the C7+9. The F°resolves nicely to the F6 (the D♭ moves up to the D (6th), A♭ up to A, D down to C, and the F is a common tone).

Three-note Answers

I established a three-note motif in the intro, and will want to continue to develop that idea throughout the arrangement both in the foreground (melody) and background (accompaniment). This is something I do intuitively. At letter **A** the answers are as follows:

Saxes:	3 notes
Trombones:	3 notes
Trombones:	1 note
Trombones/bari:	3 notes

The 3-note sax answer to the unison melody at **A** is voiced using two different configurations; spread voicings (chorale style), and Drop 3. The C7+9 has the root on the bottom and omits the 5th. It moves in contrary motion to the Gm7-5/C, which is in Drop 3. The F° is also Drop 3. The D♭ replaces the C♭ (the chord tone just below it).

The three-note bone answer in **A3-4** is especially effective. It uses open triads in the bones moving down and up chromatically while the unison alto/trumpet melody hangs on the 6th of the F chord and the 7th of the E7. The bones get to make a noble statement while the alto/trumpet unison adds some nice color.

When the saxes join the alto/trumpet unison rhythmic figure providing harmony below in **A5-6**, the bones also reverse roles and play a one-note unison. In **A7** the texture returns to that of **A3**, but this time the bari plays the roots on the bottom, and the bones are voiced in tight harmony just below the unison alto and trumpet. Also the 3-note answer moves up and down (the inversion of **A3**). Although the rhythms are the same in **A3** and **A7**, the textures and directions are opposite.

Passing Diminished Chords in 4-part Harmony

The brass takes over the melody in **A7**. This ascending line is the inversion of our descending scale motif. Notice the chromatic passing tone in the pick-up to **B**. This is subtle, but effective.

Although I have seven brass at my disposal, I use just four for this passage; two trumpets and two bones in 4-part close harmony for **A7-B2**. The voicings use no tensions except for the 9th on the G9 and the -9 on the C7-9. This final C7-9 is interesting in that it contains no 7th.

Also, the contour of each of the four parts and their relationship to the other parts lead us gracefully into the return of the alto/trumpet section. From the Gm7 to the C7-9, the 1st Trumpet ascends, the 3rd Trumpet repeats his note, Trombone 1 ascends and Trombone 3 descends, so we get contrary motion between the outer parts and a combination of contrary, parallel, and oblique motion between the other parts.

The 4-part harmony sounded fresh and interesting to me, so I felt no need to make the chords any more dense or dissonant. The final C7-9 contains the only prime dissonance (major 7th), which occurs between the outer voices. The C in the top part and the D♭ in the bottom resolve on the next measure to a D unison in the alto and trumpet.

The trumpet/alto combination makes its re-entrance at **B3**, but only for 3 measures. They

play the descending 4-note diatonic scale motif twice, the first time starting on the downbeat, and the second time starting on beat 2. The trombones answer the first statement and set up the second using only a 2-note figure. The trumpet and alto hold a unison A (the 3rd of an F chord).

In order to move smoothly to the D7, I precede it with a dominant 7th a half step above (E♭7). This makes the unison A the colorful +11 of the E♭7. The bottom two bones play the 3rd and 7th of both chords, resolving in the normal chromatic way. The 1st Trombone plays repeated F's. The first F is the 9th of E♭7 and the second F is the +9 of D7. The repeated notes create an impediment to the forward motion and make oblique motion with the lower two bones.

Shifting Gears in the Rhythm Section

The rhythm section adds to this impediment by breaking on the D7. This brings special attention to the repeat of the downward motif with its rhythmic displacement. Notice that the rhythm section has been in four for the first 3 measures of letter **B**. They break on the fourth bar, and then go into two for bars **B5-6**, only to return to four on **B7** with the reprise

of the long/short quarter notes.

Displaced Charleston

The next melody note in the song is a whole note F that should occur on the downbeat of **B6**. Instead of giving it to the trumpet and alto who are playing the melody in unison, I pass it over to the lead alto on the *and* of beat

4 (the anticipation of beat 1 of the next measure) and voice the saxes underneath using a Db/G rather than a normal G7 voicing. The saxes also play a G13sus4 just before it on beat 3 (creating a displaced Charleston rhythm—just like in the intro). Note the voice leading for those two sax chords; the top three notes ascend while the bari stays on the G (oblique motion).

Sequencing the Motif

While all this is going on in the saxes, the remaining three trumpets play a slightly altered five-note descending scale pattern starting on the *and* of beat 2, which is followed by a four-note descending altered scale in the unison trombones starting on beat 2 of the next measure. Although the harmonies in **B3-6** are interesting, it's the unpredictable rhythms that make this passage surprising, even after many listens. How many notes are there in each figure, and what beat does each figure start on? The listener understands what we are doing because we keep the same shape to the line (descending scales).

The Two Opposing Motifs

By now it is pretty obvious that this piece revolves around two opposing motifs: *motif a:* the descending major scale in eighth notes (**A2-3**) and *motif b:* the ascending long/short quarters also ascending stepwise up the major scale (**B1-2**). I juxtapose the two motifs in **B7** and **B8**. Although the melody (1st Trumpet) in **B7** repeats a set of ascending 4ths, the fact that they are long/short quarters reminds us of *motif b,* while the descending four-note diatonic figure in **B8** reminds us of *motif a* even though it's a syncopated rhythm.

Add to this the rhythm section going into four (giving us forward motion), and the unison

saxes holding out the dominant, which creates a strong pull for the resolution on the return of the *a* section of the song at letter **C**. I had the saxes enter on the *and* of beat 1 in **B7** to add accent and forward motion from the syncopation. So often, arrangers use stock figures for turnarounds—it's much stronger to use motivic material such as this.

[Let's look at and listen to **3-2: (A-C)**. Follow the motifs and how they are passed around, altered, displaced, etc. Notice how the bass relates to what's going on in the horns. Is there enough space for the rhythm section to function much like it does in a trio setting?]

To Repeat or Not To Repeat— That is the Question.

We are now at the return of the *a* section of this *abab'* form. Many times arrangers will just repeat the first *a* section and the beginning of the *b* section as far as the melody is the same as the first *b* section—especially if the original sections are complicated, sophisticated, unusual or at least interesting. Although I think letter **A** is all of those things, I've decided to go in a different direction; straight ahead 4/4 swing. More specifically, a sax soli that, although the harmonies are more sophisticated than swing era sax solis, the orchestration, melody and rhythms could be right out of 1938.

5-part Sax Soli Writing

There are two ways to harmonize a melody. You can write accompaniment in counterpoint to the melody, or you can write harmony parts with the same rhythm as the melody (*soli* or *tutti*). In jazz scoring *tutti* usually means 4-part close writing doubled throughout the sections. *Solis* are generally written using

CREATIVE JAZZ COMPOSING AND ARRANGING

thickened line voicings, but they can also involve some chorale style voicings.

Thickened lines are voiced from the melody down, generally in close or semi-close position, and are usually rootless. Chorale style has roots on the bottom.

In the 1920s, sax sections consisted of three saxes, so the solis were in 3-part harmony. Duke Ellington started writing 4-part solis in the early 1930s. He added a fifth saxophone in 1939, and either doubled the lead part down the octave, or wrote five different notes per chord. In the late 1960s Thad Jones popularized 5-part sax solis.

Letter **C** is definitely coming out of Thad. The saxes are voiced in 3rds with occasional 4ths and 2nds. I set up specific voicings for the long notes and also for notes that are accented. The 8th note passing tones are voiced using parallel diatonic movement (scalewise) in the inner parts since the melody was moving stepwise. I strive to make each part as melodic as possible. The only contrary motion occurs going into the final note of the soli (**C7**). This makes this last voicing sound special.

Unison Trombone Counterpoint

While the saxes play the harmonized melody at **C**, the bones play a unison countermelody. Notice how the bones are active while the saxes hold notes or rest, and vice versa. The idea was to give the bones a chromatically altered inversion of *motif a*, staying away from the rhythms and melody in the saxes. The successive quarter note triplets give the illusion of 3/4 being superimposed over the 4/4 meter. The pitches are derived from the E♭7 scale for Gm7-5, F° scale for F°, and the normal F major scale for the F chord.

The line starts on middle C and ascends to the G in **C3** while the saxes are descending. The bones then descend while the saxes ascend in **C4-5**. The bones rest while the saxes are active in **C5-6** and then return for their final statement using the diminished scale over the G7-9, ending on the -5, which sounds fresh since it is not in the sax voicing. This 5-part sax/unison bone texture is reminiscent of a similar section in the head of Thad Jones' wonderful *Mean What You Say*.

Once you've established your curve ball, sneak a fastball by the hitter.

Or, now that you think I'm going to keep introducing new material, it's a surprise to bring back the first 4 bars of the original *b* section. Repeating material helps the listener to understand the form and relate to the music. The style of this piece demands enough surprises to offset the regularity of the *abab'* form.

Adding Dissonance for the Final Dominant of the Head

In **D5-6**, rather than repeat the trumpet and trombone answers from **B5-6**, I want to do something special, but still subtle. The short/long quarters in **D5** remind us of our *motif b* (very truncated). The long A note in **D6** is the first note of our *motif a*. This combination of these two motifs at this critical spot in the form is most satisfying.

To add to the moment and create more pull to the tonic resolution that we expect in the next measure, I use a series of three dissonant voicings: G13sus4 with a major 3rd on top, D♭/G with the root and 5th in the top two trumpets, and finally C13sus4-9 with a major 3rd in the 3rd Trumpet part. Play the top trumpet part along with the bass. Now play the bottom trumpet, trombones and bari parts together.

Now add the upper trumpet parts. Although the upper two parts create dissonances with lower inside parts, the integrity of each part prevails and justifies the dissonances. At this point we demand resolution.

Elision

I first learned about elision in French class in seventh grade. If a word *ends* in a vowel and the next word *starts* with a vowel, lop off the vowel at the end of the first word and run the first word into the second. It took me a few years to realize that I could sometimes do this in music.

A typical spot in standard songs is when the final cadence occurs on the penultimate measure (31), and the final tonic is held for 2 bars. Most jazz musicians will use a turnaround in bars 31-32. Sometimes it is effective to lop off those 2 bars and go directly to the tonic chord at the top of the next chorus. You can't mess with the form like this when you are playing tunes at a jam session, but when you are the arranger, this sort of thing becomes very appealing.

Rather than finishing up the chorus or moving on to the top of the next chorus, I bring back the first 4 bars of the intro at letter **E**. It's familiar material containing the three-note version of our a motif, and it is clearly outside of the song form signaling that it is an interlude and will be serving to set up the next section of the piece.

The Asymmetrical Interlude

Many years ago I read liner notes by Horace Silver, in which he said that he loved creating sections of pieces that felt like they were of symmetrical length but were actually asymmetrical (7 bars, 9 bars, etc). I knew immediately that he was onto something. This

goes along with the concept of hiding dissonance that Brookmeyer laid on me.

I usually don't want my music to sound weird—I'm not big on "science projects." I love the blues, standards, jazz chord progressions and voicings. I don't want to abandon those things, but I do want to push the envelope just enough to satisfy my need for urgency.

Whereas letter **D** was shortened to 6 measures, the interlude (letter **E**) is 7 bars long. While the saxes and rhythm section play the fifth bar of the intro, the octave unison brass play two alterations of the inverted 3-note version of *motif a,* each one ending on C, the dominant.

The ensemble hits the *and* of beat 4 together, rests on the downbeat of **E6** and then plays a dramatic 7-beat dominant chord with a *fp* and a *crescendo* that leads us into the alto sax solo at the top of the next chorus. Both the drums and the alto solo fill up these seven beats to give us a preview of what's to come.

The C7-9 voicing in the brass is normal in the trumpets—from the bottom up: 7, -9, 3, 13. The trombones are a bit on the unusual side. Arrangers generally give the bones 1, 3, 5, 7 or some variation and maybe give the trumpets the 9ths, 11ths, and 13ths. Since in this case, the trumpets are covering the 3rd and 7th, rather than double them in the bones, I gave the top two trombones the root and 5th, which would be extremely grounded and obvious if trombone 3 didn't have the -5. The -5 is a real wild card. It implies tritone substitution and creates a minor 9 interval with the 1st Trombone and a tritone with the 2nd Trombone. The resulting trombone sonority is very unstable. This, combined with the stable sonority (A major triad) in the top three trumpets, is a most interesting dissonance that begs to be resolved.

[This is the end of the exposition. Listen to the entire chart up to this point, **3-3: Intro to Alto Solo (mm1-F)**. Hopefully you will be dying to find out how this story develops and the conflict is resolved.]

Solos and Backgrounds

Since so much was going on in the head, and the solo section was preceded by a loud chord, it seems fitting that we do the opposite to start the solo section; just alto sax solo with the rhythm section for the first chorus. I kept the dominant pedals on beats 2 and 4 in **G1-2** and **I1-2**. These help to define the form.

Back To Basics

When I boil this song down to its basic pitches (eliminating passing tones, etc.), it is very simple. Here is how I hear it *(Example 3-4)*:

This is the basic form I am hearing. These are the road markers, the DNA of the song. I intuitively boil materials down to the essential building blocks and then dress them up as we go along. For me, this whole song is about two notes: A and D. It's a descending perfect 5th, but also it is the sweet 3rd of the tonic key moving to the happy and wonderful 6th. Every pitch has its corresponding emotion; the same goes for chord sonorities.

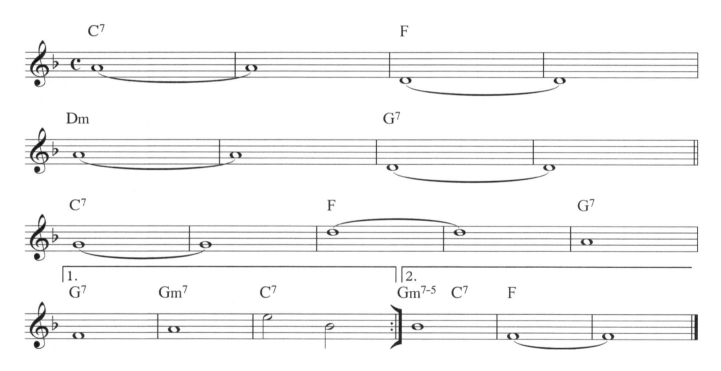

Example 3-4. Basic pitches

Keeping the Soloists on Track

One of the challenges in jazz performance is improvising solos that, while being creative, also serve to develop the material of the song; developing the motifs in the exposition to move toward a satisfying climax. Left to their own devices, the soloists and rhythm section might stray from the arranger's conception. Written backgrounds help to rein everyone in and keep them on the path.

Simplify

In order to leave the soloist space, not step on his toes or put him in a straitjacket, I generally try to keep the backgrounds from getting too note-y. Very often I use longer note values, rests, and rhythmic figures that will leave plenty of space for the soloists to create their lines.

Defining the Form

The rhythmic scheme to this *abab'* form is that the *a* section, which centers around the pitches A and D, and moves between them in descending stepwise 8th notes, while the *b* section negotiates its ascending 5th in stepwise half notes. I'm going to use this as the basis for the backgrounds for the alto solo.

Writing for Six Brass

The backgrounds are played the second time only and, since the soloist is in the reed section, the backgrounds for this chorus are assigned to the brass. Using the opposite choir from the soloist helps the listener to distinguish between foreground and background. The 2nd Trumpet will be soloing the next chorus, so I have omitted him from these backgrounds, leaving three trumpets and three trombones available for the background.

Unisons Within the Voicings

Nearly every chord has six different pitches. When there are only five different pitches, I double two of the voices, and then move away from the unison in contrary motion, so that we don't lose the illusion of 6-part harmony. There are no octave doublings in this chorus.

Appropriate Ranges and Dynamics for Backgrounds

I often hear pianists indiscriminately comping in their upper register, which distracts us from the soloist. Backgrounds, for the most part, should be subservient to the soloist. There may be moments of call-and-response where the background temporarily becomes the foreground, but mostly, we don't want to be confused as to who is primary. To use a football analogy: who are the blockers, and who is carrying the ball?

Similarly, when writing horn backgrounds, if you keep them in the low or middle register, they won't compete for attention with the soloist. The same goes for dynamics. Most modern bands play everything loud, which forces the soloist to play as loud as he can, swallowing a microphone in the bell of his instrument and resulting in a very loud, distorted sound. If backgrounds are written in the proper register at a low volume, soloists should be able to play the full dynamic range of their instrument without any amplification.

That said, backgrounds should be interesting both melodically and harmonically. Although you probably won't want them to be disruptive, in most cases there should be a rhythmic payoff.

Background Motifs

The rhythms in letter **F** are developed out of the displaced Charleston rhythm of the intro (quarter note on beat 3, 8th rest on beat

4, and 8th note on the *and* of beat 4, which is tied over to a whole note). **F1-2** is our intro rhythm minus the first quarter note. **F3-4** is the motif plus the starting quarter on beat 3 of **F4**. **F5-6** is a Charleston rhythm (with an added note in the 2nd Trombone) followed by a retrograde version of our displaced Charleston. **F7** is a slight alteration of the retrograde of our figure.

If we look at the pitches in the lead trumpet part at **F**, we have our central motif (A, D) followed by C, A, C, A. The C functions as an alteration of the D (alterations generally change notes by a minor or major 2nd). Also, the D is an octave higher, so that the motif is inverted. Similarly, the repeated E in measure **F7** is an alteration of the D (a whole step higher).

Brass Voicings

I pretty much think of the brass as one section when they play together, although I do try to give both the trumpets and the trombones sonorities that will feel good within their respective sub-sections. Very often, when writing for brass, the bones will have the lower partials of the chords, and the trumpets will have the upper—but not always. I try to mix this up, so that the voicings deliver subtle surprises for the players as well as the listeners.

The first voicing at **F** sets the mood and *mp* dynamic. The 3rd Trombone has the root. This chord is functionally a dominant in the key of F. I might have called it C13sus4-9. I call it Gm7-5/C to facilitate faster reading in the rhythm section. The 2nd Trombone has the 5th (G), and then I build the chord up in 3rds. Horns generally sound comfortable and full when voiced in 3rds. So, on this voicing from the bottom up: the bones have root, 5th and 7th (lower partials) while the trumpets have

the upper partials -9, 11 and 13. Each subsection has an interesting and pleasing sonority.

The voicing on beat 3 of **F3** has the bones in 5ths and the trumpets in 4ths together making an F69. The top two trumpets are in unison, which is a bit unusual. I didn't hear any other notes in the voicing and I like the line created for Trumpet 3. I don't feel a need for contrary motion, since this voicing is followed by a rest. The next voicing has the top two bones in unison. They do depart in contrary motion. Everyone descends from the E7 to the Eb7 except for Trombone 1, who ascends into a minor 2nd with Trumpet 4. So, the trumpet doubling in **F3** is then passed to the bones in **F4**.

Upper-structure Triads

Ever since Thad Jones' popularity in the late 1960s, jazz arrangers have been on a steady diet of upper-structure triads in the trumpets. For me, this gets tiresome. I like variety and surprises. I have nothing against upper-structure triads—in fact I use them often—but I like to mix them up with other sonorities. Let's look at the first seven voicings in letter **F**:

A+/C7, 4ths/F, 4ths/E7, A+/Eb7, open cluster/A7, Dm9, E/G7

The only recognizable upper-structure is the final E/G7, which makes a G13-9. It's our sweet reward for waiting.

Pyramids

The bottom two bones create a pyramid effect with the other four brass in **F5**. The D on the bottom states the root of the tonic Dm chord, ignores the A7 (the dominant of Dm) and continues to hold through the Dm7. I will develop this idea of building dominant chords over tonics as this chart progresses. The G in the 2nd Trombone creates a 4th with the bottom voice, and is also the 11th of the Dm and Dm7 chords and the 7th of the A7. 4ths on the bottom of the bone voicings are a reflection of all the 4ths in the trumpet voicings. The individual pyramid entrances will need to be developed in order to satisfy us, but you are going to have to wait until letter **G**.

Since the bottom two bones are acting as independent parts (with their own rhythms), this leaves the 1st Trombone to join the trumpets, and essentially act as a fourth trumpet in **F5-6**. The Dm7 voicing has the top four voices forming a traditional 4-way close Dm9 voicing (C,E,F,A). This voicing is approached in contrary motion with the top voice descending, the second voice repeating his note, and the bottom two voices ascending. Notice the oblique motion between the second and third voices that results in a minor 2nd These kinds of things make background parts fun to play for horn players.

Top To Bottom

Starting with the pick-up to **G**, the melody of the song appears (slightly altered) in the 1st Trombone. The three trumpets are voiced in close harmony above him using the same passing diminished chords as on the head. In **F1-2** the bottom two trombones play dominant pedals on beats two and four. The pick-up to **G** has the bottom bones playing a G, which is the dominant of the upcoming C pedal. The integrity of the two harmonic schemes and their ultimate resolution to the tonic in **G3** builds some intriguing tension. The C pedals are doubled in the bass and serve as signposts in the form.

The arrival on the tonic in **G3** is celebrated by the bottom two bones joining the rest of the brass to form 6-part voicings and the trumpets forming an upper-structure triad (C/F6).

The Eb13 on beat 3 is a bit more condensed and crunchy. It expands in both directions into an interesting D7 voicing. The solid root is in the melody, but directly below is the -5 and the +9 in the trumpets. The tritone between the top two voices creates an uneasiness with the melody in the trumpet. The bones have the normal 7th and 3rd, but instead of the root on the bottom, I used the -9.

Notice that both the trumpet section and the trombone section have the same spacings; a tritone and a minor 3rd. This creates a symmetrical voicing built on the diminished scale. I like symmetrical voicings whether they contain the same structure (like this one) or mirror inversion. To make this into a mirror inversion, we could just give the 2nd Trombone an A rather than an F#.

Syncopation vs. On the Beat

While letter **F**'s rhythms were all about syncopation, the first 5 bars of **G** are all on the beat. The change in the rhythmic scheme helps everyone to understand the form. Trombone 3 continues his independent pedal function on the third beat of **G5**, but then holds it over into **G6**, where he joins the rest of the brass section as they go back to syncopated figures similar to letter **F**. These 6-part voicings are crunchier than the previous ones.

The Turnaround

Normally turnarounds will resolve to the first chord of the next section through the dominant of that chord. However it sometimes happens that the last chord of the bridge of a 32-bar *aaba* song will be the dominant of the key, even if the first chord of the upcoming *a* section is a chord other than the tonic. This happens in *Perdido;* the last change in the bridge is F7 (the dominant in Bb) although the first bar of the return of the *a* section is Cm7.

The same situation can be present in *abab'* forms such as **Do It Again**. So although the first chord at **H** is a C7, the last chord of the turnaround in **G8** is also a C7. I've used a typical *iii V/ii ii V* (Am7 D7 Gm7 C7) progression for the turnaround, which contains very stable, tonal harmonies. The melody in the 1st Trumpet is a retrograde Lydian mode variation of the original 5-note diatonic motif. Each melody note gets its own chord. The bass plays quarter notes rather than going with the syncopations in the horns. Since the harmonies and inner parts are moving quickly and jumping intervals, the quarters in the bass provide needed stability.

Each chord has six different pitches, with the exception of the C7-9 on the *and* of beat 3. For this voicing, I have doubled the melody note E (the 3rd of the chord) at the octave in the 4th Trumpet. This octave doubling exaggerates the dissonance of the sus4 (2nd Trombone) and the 3rd as well as the tritone between the B♭ in Trombone 1 and the E in Trumpet 4. This is an odd voicing that I don't recall ever using before or since, but I quite like it in this spot.

Note that the rhythm and shape of this turnaround is a syncopated version of the first four notes of **A4-5**, which itself is the inversion of the pitches of **A2-3** (our *motif a* minus the starting note).

Using Accidentals Judiciously

I once taught a class called **Titans of the Tenor**, where I transcribed and analyzed solos by about 100 of the greatest tenor saxophonists in the history of jazz. After looking at transcriptions of dozens of Lester Young's solos, I was struck by how few accidentals he played per chorus—an average of three—and they almost always were blue notes in the key (♭3, ♭5 and ♭7). I then started looking at standard songs. They too used a minimum of accidentals with a predominance of blue notes.

Diatonic melodies are very singable. They add simplicity and orderliness. Blue notes add the flavor of the blues—even when they occur in bass lines and inside parts. Let's look at the first 7 bars of letter **H**. There are only 18 accidentals out of 120 notes in the brass (15%). Of those 18 accidentals, 15 are blue notes (83%). This passage doesn't strike me as being particularly bluesy, but the numbers don't lie. Of course sometimes the music is more chromatic than others (my bebop-oriented sax solis are crazy with accidentals—you can check out *No Refill* and *A Whole New You* on my **Hindustan** CD), but in general, clarity is a very worthwhile pursuit.

Rhythm is the most powerful tool in our toolbox.

The rhythmic construction of letter **H** is very interesting. It starts with the long (4-beat) syncopated note like **F1**, only now it starts a measure earlier in the form and adds two short syncopated punctuations (two beats apart). This figure is followed by the same rhythm as **F8-G1** and the beginning of **G2**. I'm condensing the rhythms of letter **F** and **G**, putting them side-by-side.

H5-8 is a development of the rhythm of **G8**. I use the rhythm of the four notes of **G8** and then repeat the first three notes. After a quarter rest, I repeat the first five notes of **H5-6**, except that I put an 8th note in front of it, thus making it a 6-note figure. Notice the use of the blue notes in Trumpet 1 and Trombone 1. They add a sweet surprise. Also the dissonance of the minor 2nds between the 2nd and 3rd Trumpet, and the minor 9th between the 1st Trumpet and the 2nd Trombone, add to the percussiveness of these rhythms.

Repeating Signposts Verbatim

The first 2 bars of the *b* sections of this song are always accompanied by backbeat dominant pedals, so that no matter how far out our *a* sections get, we always know where we are when we get to the *b* section. These pedals serve as signposts. It can be effective to repeat signposts verbatim, so that they are clear. Perhaps my favorite example of this is the one-bar send-off figure in Al Cohn's *Some Of My Best Friends*. The distinctive rhythm with the +11 in the melody snaps us to attention like smelling salts.

In this tradition, **H8-I3** are direct repeats *(come sopra)* of **F8-G3**. Now that we are all comfortable with familiar material, it's time for a few surprises. **I4** starts with an unusual symmetrical voicing. Both the trumpets and bones have a tritone on top of a minor 3rd. The tritone between the top two trumpets is extremely volatile.

Time for Some Fun

The following two voicings are no less unusual. Normally we would harmonize the A on the third beat as a D7 (the dominant of the upcoming Dm7/G or, functionally, G7sus4). But since we already sounded a D7 on the previous note, I'm going to try a different approach. An obvious choice could be F♯°, which would give us good bass movement, but doesn't relieve the repetition in the upper voices.

The same goes for A♭7, although I do like the contrary motion between the 1st Trumpet and the bottom trombone. The minor 9th dissonance between these parts is quite pronounced. By voicing the Dm7/G with 4ths in the bones and 5ths in the trumpets, we arrive at a very stable and yet most interesting sonority. The next step is to voice-lead everyone except the top voice chromatically downward,

so that the A in the 1st Trumpet is the -9 on the A♭7sus4 and the B♮ is the major 3rd on the G7sus4. Let's take three beats rest to let this voicing ring while we digest it.

Repeating the Send-off

Remember the send-off to the alto sax solo from two choruses ago—the 7-beat C13-9 starting on beat 2 of **E6**? In **E5** we use a longer dominant chord (13 beats) and start it on a different syncopation (*scronch* on the fourth beat). This time it's a sus4 chord with an interesting voicing—an A major triad in the trumpets over 4ths in the bones. This chord has a dual function. It signals the end of the alto solo and ushers in the trumpet. Notice the upward whole-step motion in the lead trumpet to arrive at this important chord. This whole-step motion was introduced by the saxes at the end of the intro and will be developed further in future choruses.

[Now listen to this background chorus **3-4: Bgds of Alto Solo (F-J 2nd X)**. For a background, there is a lot going on here. Hopefully it is rich, but not distracting from the soloist. After listening a few times, go back to the top of the chart and listen to **3-5: Intro to Tpt Solo (mm1-J)**. I'm gently pushing the motifs forward to keep the soloist from straying too far from the feeling of the chart.]

Trumpet Solo with Backgrounds

6-part Saxophone/Trombone Voicings

For the first 30 bars of the 32-bar trumpet solo, the backgrounds are written for four saxes and two trombones in 6-part harmony. A few of their notes are in unison, but they quickly break out into 6-part harmony. Since the soloist is a trumpet, I chose the saxes (the opposing choir) to predominate in the backgrounds. Although there are two bones in the voicings, they are inside, so that they serve to add mostly harmonic, plus a little orchestrational, color.

The 2nd Alto is *tacet* for this chorus, so that he doesn't have to jump from his solo directly into playing ensemble. I only needed two trombones, so I chose to let the 1st Trombone sit this chorus out. I was looking more for the other trombonists' personalities. Also, the lead trombone chair is taxing on the chops, so it's good to give him some rest when I can. The general formula for this chorus is to intersperse the bones among the saxes in this order:

> Alto 1
> Trombone 1
> Tenor 3
> Trombone 3
> Tenor 4
> Bari

Creating a Contrasting Background Out of the Same Motifs

At **J** the trumpet soloist has 3 bars alone with the rhythm section to establish himself. This respite from horn backgrounds serves to cleanse the palate before we embark on the next course. **J5-8** is the rhythm of **G8-H1** but using the pitches of the 4-note descending diatonic motif from the intro. The first two pitches are octave unisons. The next two voicings set the tone for this entire chorus; dense, no vibrato, pale colored sonorities that are abundant in 4th intervals, resulting in many sus4 chords and variations. However there are a few bluesy voicings interspersed, like the A7-9 in **J4**. It also contains a +9 and +5. This colorful chord is short-lived. A beat later the Dm7 introduces the predominant sound of this chorus. You could call it a Cmaj7/D, which is pretty much how it functions. Another way to look at it is a series of 4ths. From the bottom up: A, D, G, C, and another set of 4ths: B♭ and E.

Do you remember the *scronch* in **I5-8**? It returns in **J6-8**; however the pitches have been changed to protect the innocent.* The top voice in the alto merely repeats the previous chord, which gives us continuity. The unusual thing about this chord is that, instead of using a +11, there is a ♮11th in the 1st Trombone rubbing against the 3rd in the top tenor. This sonority is similar to the previous Dm7 except for the F and A♭, which give it a darker color.

Passing Diminished/Pedal Point

The character of the *b* section of this song is greatly enhanced by the passing diminished chord (F#°) on the third beat of **B1**. It is set up by an A°/G on the fourth beat of **A8**. This repeats 16 measures later. In the next chorus, the pick-up is preserved, but a dominant pedal point (C's in the bass) is added on beats two and four. This also repeats 16 measures later.

When we get to our third chorus at **K**, the pick-up is preserved, but the dominant pedal point has been omitted. On the F#° in **K1**, the G at the bottom of the previous and upcoming Gm7 is retained (and re-struck) . The effect of this is a G tonic pedal below the *vii°*. The alto melody in **J8-K4** retains the same rhythm and shape as the previous chorus but on different notes of the scale. **K3** reverses the order of the C, A of the previous chorus and resolves to the same D (also with a volatile tritone interval in the second voice).

Perfect Intervals vs. Diminished and Augmented Intervals

Starting at **K1**, the first Gm7 is built in 4ths with a 5th on top (G, C, F, B♭ then D, A). The next Gm7 is built in 5ths (G, D, A then B♭, F,

*To quote the long-running radio and tv series *Dragnet.*

C). The Fmaj7 in the next bar is built in 4ths on the bottom and 5ths on top (F, C, G and B, E, A). The prevalence of chords built in 4ths and 5ths is related to the outside notes of the 4-note motif (A scale-wise down to E) and the 5-note motif (A down to D). The vertical expression of horizontal ideas is subtle but powerful.

The remaining chords from this passage have varied structures. The F#° has a G on the bottom, two sets of tritones and a B on top (G, C, F#, A, E♭, B). The C9+5 is constructed of two augmented triads (C, E, G# and F#, A#, D) utilizing all six notes of the whole-tone scale. The E♭9 has an upper-structure triad over minor 3rds (F, A, C over G, B♭, D♭). The volatile D7-9 has a tritone over a diminished 7th, or it could be taken apart as three pairs of tritones (F# and C, A and E♭, A♭ and D).

The next phrase starts in unison, spreads into a 4ths voicing, ducks back into a unison for one note and then lands on a juicy G13-9+11. The lead alto starts with the inversion of the five-note diatonic motif. After leaving some space for the trumpet soloist, the background in **K7-8** returns to the descending whole-tone motif from the end of the intro, only this time it is harmonized with an altered traditional turnaround: Am11 D7sus4-9 Gm11 C13sus4-9. Notice the prevalence of 4th and 5th intervals in these voicings. The D7sus4-9 also has an added major 3rd to rub against the sus4. I have spelled these chords differently for the pianist, for the sake of simplicity in reading. The syncopations from **K5-8** are played long as opposed to the short syncopations in the intro.

The Return of the Charleston from the Intro

Note that the last note in **K8** (which is tied over into **L**) is unison. This helps us under-

stand **K5-8** as a unit (starting and ending with unison) and also leaves space for the piano to comp in **L1-4**. I've given the entire rhythm section two displaced Charleston figures, which remind us of the first 2 bars of the intro.

The B♮ in the lead alto in **K7-8** (which is derived from the intro) is the -5 (a blue note) in the key of F. It also establishes the Lydian mode. It might be fun to exploit this. In **L5-8** the alto hangs onto this B♮, which is dissonant against the Dm7 and Dm7-5/G harmonies. The E that precedes it (fourth beat of **L4**) is a 5th below. By now we realize that a large part of the sonority of this chart is 4th and 5th vertical intervals within the voicings. It's nice in this spot to hear the 5th expressed horizontally.

Added to that, the A7-9 is voiced from the bottom up: A, D and G (4ths), then minor 3rds above the G: B♭, C# and E. The D (11th) is the unusual note, but this 4th voicing was well established before this chorus. Similarly, the Dm7 is voiced in 4ths (A, D, G and C) with a 5th above (E and B). The Dm7-5/G is functionally a G7sus4-9. It's voiced in 5ths (G, D, A♭, E and B). The A♭ is a chromatic modal alteration of the A that would be diatonic. It creates more pull to the resolution on **M1**. I've also added a C in the voicing to continue the sus4 sonority.

Minor 13 Chords and Sus4 chords with Major 3rds

Although it is somewhat unusual to use 13ths on minor 7th chords that resolve down a 5th to a dominant 7th, and both the sus4 and the major 3rd in dominant 7th voicings, the character of this piece seemed to call out for these sounds. These chords appear often. This repetition makes these sounds seem more and more normal.

Returning to the Signpost

M1-2 has the dominant pedals on beats two and four that we used as a signpost in earlier choruses. This time it's just in the rhythm section (like the piano solo at the top of the chart). It's nice to have a relief from the thick sax/bone voicings.

More Sus4 Chords with a Different Twist

M4-6 is similar to 8 bars before, even though it is in a different place in the song. I love when this happens. Although the B♮ and E are in the lead alto, their order is reversed. I've added an A♭ (another blue note) pick-up, which is voiced as a D7-9: 3, 5, 7, -9 with the +9 and +11 on top. This voicing is rootless and in close position. It jumps in contrary motion to the Dm7/G (functionally a G13sus4), which is spread out wide. Notice the E and F (a minor 2nd interval) near the bottom, and the A and B (major 2nd) between the top two voices. The following Gm7-5/C functions as a C7sus4-9. It's voiced in 4ths (G, C, F, B♭, E) with an added D♭ to darken it.

Staggered Entrances, or the Unison Pyramid

As the trumpet solo comes to its final cadence, the saxes and bones play a syncopated, octave unison tonic. The remaining trumpets and trombone repeat the F on successive beats. This technique serves to close this section and signal that a new section is about to start. The 3rd Trumpet is the last one to sound his note, and to not be complacent, he plays his note a whole step higher. This set of staggered entrances sets up the shout chorus in a dramatic fashion.

[Let's listen to the trumpet solo chorus **3-6: Tpt Solo (J-N)**. Then listen to the two solo choruses with backgrounds. See how the motifs of this piece are nudged along without forcing the soloists into a corner. Then listen from the top through the end of the trumpet solo. Do you feel the tension building and the need for an explosive shout chorus? If there were any doubt, the final crescendo in the drums puts that to rest.]

The always swinging Jimmy Madison.

The Shout Chorus

Big band jazz was initially created to accompany social dancers. The typical arrangement reached its climax about ¾ of the way through the chart. Since climaxes are most obvious when they are louder and more intense than the rest of the chart, the horn players shout out their rhythms; hence the term *shout chorus*. Sometime later it became fashionable to precede the *shout* with a *soft shout*. Ellington's masterpiece, *Harlem Airshaft* (1940) predates the New Testament Count Basie Orchestra's soft shouts by 15 years.

Bebop/Big Band Dilemma

When bebop was developing in the early 1940s, it was seen as being in opposition to swing, even though it was a natural outgrowth of its predecessor. Aside from its rhythmic, melodic and harmonic innovations, bebop was largely improvised small group music as opposed to swing music, which was mainly elaborately arranged big band music. Since big bands had prestige and commercial appeal, there were early attempts to present bebop in big band settings. In most cases concessions were made, so that these pieces were essentially swing charts with some bebop elements. This is true of both the Billy Eckstine and Dizzy Gillespie big bands.

The Solution

Oddly enough it was the "sweet" white band of Claude Thornhill that came up with the most satisfying big band bebop arrangements, in the sense that they were truest to the bebop aesthetic. Gil Evans' charts grew out of both the "cool school" of Lester Young and the bebop of Charlie Parker and Dizzy Gillespie. Gone are the sax solis and the call-and-response between sections. The harmonies are denser and more abstract. The colors are paler; less vivid. No more Louis Armstrong vibrato.

Gil's friendship with Miles Davis led to the **Birth Of The Cool** and later to the four albums they collaborated on for Columbia, starting with **Miles Ahead**. Gil's influence can be heard in the writing of John Lewis, John Carisi, Gerry Mulligan, J.J. Johnson, Bob Brookmeyer, and later on, Chuck Israels.

(Although Maria Schneider was a disciple of Gil's, her music eschews bebop, swing and the blues. This is true to different degrees for some later Brookmeyer and many of his students. This abandonment of much of the jazz tradition may be rooted partly in Gil's interest in pop music with his later band in the 1970s. In fact, Gil and many other jazz musicians of the swing era, saw themselves as popular musicians, so when popular music went in another direction, they attempted to stay current even though the new music was the younger generation's rebellion against the sophistication of jazz.)

I first became aware of Gil's arrangements in 1964 when I borrowed a copy of **Miles Ahead** from a friend. Later that year, my aunt bought me **Birth Of The Cool**. I was 15 and those records had a profound effect on me. When we are young, we are open to new things, and when we feel an affinity, these things become a part of us. And so it was for me. I had a pretty firm grasp of swing bands like Basie's, but Gil's approach was much more subtle and elusive. I saw hot jazz and cool jazz as the range of jazz expression, rather than as mutually exclusive. I wanted my music to embody both.

Later, when I was working for Gil, I asked him about his aesthetic. His reply was that he was just trying to sound like Billy Strayhorn. Of course Gil had his own sound, but I understand what he heard in Strayhorn's music. Although Ellington influenced Strayhorn to a great degree, Strayhorn brought cooler and more European-influenced sounds to the Ellington orchestra, and inspired the Maestro to grow in that direction. Theirs was a truly symbiotic relationship. Gil went several steps further.

The Anti-Shout

Although I can't think of a single sax soli in Gil's music (*King Porter Stomp* comes the closest with its saxophone/trombone soli), his ensemble solis are crucial to the character of his music. *I Don't Want To Be Kissed* is a great example of soli writing for all the horns. The basis of this is 4-part close harmony (block chords or *tutti* voicings). Sometimes Gil adds a tuba part on the bottom that is often in contrary motion.

With this in mind, **N1-5** is scored in classic *tutti* style. I had the 1st and 2nd Trumpets *tacet* along with the 2nd Alto. They will have integral parts to play in the next phrase. This leaves me with five brass and four saxes. The brass section is voiced in 4-part close harmony, with the lead doubled down the octave in the 3rd Trombone. The saxes double the brass starting with the second voice, so that the bari doubles the 3rd Trombone (and the 3rd Trumpet down the octave). The warm sound of the bari helps to temper the bright sound of the top trumpet voice.

Like Ellington, I use *tutti* writing for note-y passages that involve brass and saxes. It is compact and has the least amount of weight while producing full harmonies. At Letter **N** I chose my anchor chords, then the passing chords, and finally I made adjustments when necessary, to get satisfying voicings and good parts for every horn. In actuality I wound up not needing to make any adjustments in this passage.

Many arrangers view 4-part close writing as formulaic, but there are really many variables; the most essential of which is the melody/bass relationship.

Displaced Rhythm Producing Asymmetrical Phrases

Using the 4- and 5-note descending diatonic scale motif, the phrase at **N** is arranged in this pattern of beats: 1 (rest), 3, 2, 4, 6 and 4. Although predominantly in 8th notes, the longer values and syncopations in this passage add to the rhythmic interest. Let's look at each of the sections of this long phrase. I'll take them in order and identify them by the number of beats.

1. This quarter rest comes as a surprise. The previous unison pyramid and crescendo makes us expect a loud chord, but instead we get silence from the horns, which creates a *subito p* signaling a soft shout chorus.

2. Our original 4-note descending diatonic motif.

3. We repeat the same four eighth notes, except that we start on the upbeat and add a fifth note, which is like our 5-note motif, only this last note is a half step lower (Db instead of D) to darken the line and conform to the Gm7-5/C.

4. This segment is a bit tricky. It is essentially a sequence of our 4-note motif. The final C, when transposed up the octave, is really the first note of the descending diatonic (F major) sequence (C, Bb, A, G).

5. This is the retrograde of the 5-note motif but continues the F major scale pattern, so that it completes the entire octave (C to C). The C# is the leading tone into Dm.

6. This final segment is the period of this first sentence. It consists of one interval (descending major 6th), the widest interval so far, which, coupled with the strong rhythm, makes a statement that we must notice. The repeated G's (*re* in the key of F) hold onto our tonality established by the previous strong G's on the downbeat of **N2** and the *and* of beat 4 in **N3**. The following phrase in the 2nd Alto and 2nd Trumpet (the return of our bebop frontline from the head) will also end on G in **N7**, which serves to set up the brass chord on the *and* of beat 4 of that measure.

4-Part Close Voicings

I wanted a smooth, flowing thickened line, so I was careful to make every part melodic without repeated pitches. Repeating a note tends to disrupt the flow. The one repeated pitch occurs purposely going from the second beat of **N4** to the syncopated note on the *and* of beat 2. This repeat signals the change from 8th notes to syncopated quarters.

The passing chords are mostly diatonic. I chose my tensions carefully for richness of sound and voice leading (melodic flow). Here is a schematic *(Example 3-5)*. Note that the rhythm section is not informed of the passing chords. The simpler their parts, the more flow. The overall effect feels like the horns are floating over the rhythm section.

As you can see, basically when the melody moves scale-wise, the harmonies move in parallel motion (with slight alterations to add harmonic interest). Some interesting spots are:

1. **N2**—the resolutions of the tonic F⁰ chords to the Fmaj9 chords.

2. The Bᶜ's in **N3-4**, which suggest F Lydian.

Hexatonic Voicings

You'll notice that on the *and* of beat 4 of **N7** the bones play an Fm triad, with the trumpets sounding an Em triad above them. The first time I noticed this structure of minor triads built at the major 7th was in the music of Alban Berg. The first usage I know of in jazz is on Clare Fischer's album ***Extensions***. Although I normally use this structure for 6-note voicings, it could be used for 4- and 5-note chords, or as chords using more than six notes. For more notes, just stack more minor triads, eg. Dm/E♭m/Em/Fm.

I generally use hexatonic voicings on dominants. The bottom minor triad can be built on the 3rd, 5th, 7th or -9 of the dominant 7th chord. So for instance, on a G7 you can use B♭m/Bm, C#m/Dm, Em/Fm or Gm/A♭m. Al-

Example 3-5. Schematic at N

though I usually build these voicings in 3rds, I sometimes spread them out and/or create half steps between notes by using octave displacement (either up or down).

This spot in **N7** gave me a great solution to a voicing problem. Generally, voicing dominants with the 3rd or 7th in the melody in the usual ways fails to satisfy me. They sound too obvious. Hexatonics add dissonant notes into the mix, but curiously (because of their symmetrical structure) sound "correct."

Another Dominant 7th Solution

Chuck Israels showed me another solution to the 3rd/7th problem. If you have a 3rd or 7th in the melody of a dominant 7th chord, you can voice a rootless dominant 7th a minor 3rd away. So for instance, if you have a G7, you can voice a B♭7 or an E7. The F melody (the 7th of G7) would become the 5th of a B♭7 and the B melody (the 3rd of G7) would become the 5th of the E7. I have used these a few times, adding 9ths and possibly 13ths and +11ths. The 9th on the B♭7 (C) gives us the 11th on the G7, and the 9th on the E7 (F♯) is the major 7th on G7. Interesting notes! Use with care.

Brass vs. Reeds

Starting at **N8** we revert to the traditional brass versus reeds formula. In this case the saxes are unison and the brass are in 6-part harmony. The saxes function as a dominant pedal (G) in **N8-O3** and then switch to D (the dominant of G) in **O4**. This sets up **O5-8**, which is basically G7. The twisty ascending lines in **N8** and **O3-4** presage the simple ascending line in **O5**, which is the retrograde of our 5-note descending scale motif, but with a chromatically altered final note. The alteration (the -9 on the G7) gives us a gentle surprise, plus it's a blue note (♭3 in the key of F).

The lead trumpet melody in **O1-3** is also the retrograde of the 5-note ascending motif with the second to last note (E♭) altered. Note that the trumpet is in the key of C (with an E♭ blue note), while the sax line is in the key of F (with an A♭ blue note). Motifs can be sequenced diatonically or chromatically (transposed to other keys). The trumpet line also has the starting A inserted in the middle of the line and repeated at the end—much like how the sax line in **N8** returns to the starting note G.

The lead trumpet line in **O4-5** is our original 4-note descending diatonic motif, except that it is transposed down a step to the key of E♭. I've used punchy, short syncopations in contrast to the legato eighth notes and long notes in the saxes.

Counterpoint is most effective when the different lines are given opposite characters.

6-part Brass Voicings

For bars **O1-5**, the top four voices (three trumpets and one trombone) are voiced in 4-part close harmony. The bottom two bones are given two pitches from the chord scales that are not being used by the top four voices. Sometimes they are unused lower chord functions such as roots and 5ths (as in the first voicing at **O1**, and sometimes they are unused upper structure tensions such as the -9 and 7 on the C7-9 chord on the *and* of beat 3 in **O2**. I have also used a G pedal on the F♯° in **O1**. Holding over the G from the previous Gm7 and coming back to it in the next measure create a logical situation for this dissonance.

There is only one sandwich chord in this passage: the C♯° on the *and* of beat 3 in **O4**. The bottom four notes of the voicing contain the basic chord sounds, while the top two trumpets sound the major 7th and 9th. The brass chord in **O6** is the first time in this passage that we hear a low root on the bottom.

The brass players are placed in their middle registers at a medium volume (*mf*). I'm building to the climax.

Don't be seduced by your lead trumpet player's ability to play high and loud. Just because he can do it, doesn't mean that he should do it all the time. Pick your spots and they will be more effective.

Combinations Involving the Bebop Frontline

The trumpet/alto bebop frontline returns one last time in **O6-P1** with an extended altered descending motif. It is followed by an ascending motif and a 4-note descending motif transposed to the key of D♭. The alto and trumpet are promptly answered by the six brass playing repeated dominant sus4 chords. The top five voices are built in 3rds, and the bottom trombone plays the root. I was looking for brightness rather than weight, so I voiced the bones tightly under the trumpets rather than putting a low anchor on the bottom.

The saxes answer in **P2-5** with a unison 5-note diatonic retrograde motif; the last note is in 4-part harmony and elides into a harmonized 4-note diatonic motif taken out of order—G, D, F, E are pitches #1, #4, #2, #3. The voicings move gradually from open position to close: Drop 3, Drop 2 and then the two final chords in 4-part close.

The unison bebop frontline dovetails the harmonized saxes and then the harmonized bones in **P5-6**, first with an ascending sequence of descending motifs, then followed by ascending and descending motifs punctuated by two low A's. The number of notes in the motifs vary: 4, 4, 3 (with a turn), 3 and 4 (with a turn).

The bones fulfill their noble role in **P5** with an A triad (the alto and trumpet unison contains the 7th and -9). In the following measure they have the unusual spacing on a Dm7 with the 7th on the bottom. This works because of the smooth voice leading and because, besides the Dm7, it suggests a second inversion F6. The alto and trumpet fill in the A (the 5th of Dm7 or 3rd of the F6).

Back to Brass vs. Reeds

The saxes hold a unison G root in **P7-8** preceded by an 8th note triplet. The triplet consists of an ascending minor 2nd and an ascending minor 3rd before dropping down a 4th to the G. I pick up the ascending 3rds in the lead trumpet. It's all diatonic (key of F) until the final B♮. We've been using this Lydian fourth step of the scale throughout the whole chart, starting with the sixth bar of the intro. We gain intensity here due to the ascending brass, the brass tessitura (lead trumpet above the staff), the punchy rhythm, the dynamics, and the dissonance of the voicings.

I start with voicing the top four brass in 4-part close harmony with added unused notes in the bottom two bones. I use this formula for the first three notes, which are G7sus4 chords. The voicing on the *and* of beat 3 uses the hexatonic voicing Em/Fm. Since the melody notes repeat the first four notes (A, C, E and G), I use the same voicings for the next four notes and repeat the fifth note, since the melody is a repeated G.

The final voicing is an F#°/G. Note that the bottom two bones double the G bass note. The G bass will resolve to a C pedal, and the F#° will resolve up to the Gm7 in the next measure (**Q1**). Also, the top two trombones cross parts in **P7** and **P8**. This occurred organically by giving the 2nd Trombone the G root, yielding interesting (and melodic) parts.

The Abbreviated Recap

Although many, if not most, jazz charts follow the shout chorus with a recapitulation, which is generally a chorus, a half chorus, or at the very least 8 bars, this chart just hints at a recap from **Q1-6** before it moves on to the coda. Actually, I didn't even realize that I was quoting the melody when I wrote this section. The saxes have taken over the melody that was previously played by the brass in **D1-4**. Instead of long/short quarters, the top four saxes play half notes while the bari answers with repeated dominant pedal 8th notes. The saxes are in Drop 2 with a passing diminished. The rhythm section reinforces the dominant pedals on beats two and four, as they have done in this part of the tune earlier in the chart.

As smoothly as the saxes ascended, in **Q3** they descend in Drop 2—F6 Am7 Gm7 E♭9-5. The final two chords are reminiscent of **D3-4** in the bones, only now scored for five saxes. The top three saxes repeat the bone voicing, and the bottom two add root and 5th near the bottom of their horns. The rhythm is different from **D3-4**, and the final D7+9 is repeated.

The trumpets answer with the unison melody (the descending 4-note motif), which is echoed in the unison bones with an added skip down to the G followed by a brass chord similar to **E6-7**. Instead of the powerful send-off, it is now *mf* and scored an octave lower. The 2nd Trombone has a D♭ this time instead of a C, and the rhythm section has G♭7-9 instead of C7-9 (the interchangeable tritone substitute).

Coda

While the brass hold their chord, the saxes play a two octave unison ascending diminished scales, first six notes and then eight, landing on a C7+5+9 voiced with an upper-structure A♭ triad over the 3rd and 7th. These ascending scales are altered and extended versions of our old friend the descending diatonic 5-note motif. While the saxes sustain their voicing, the brass reverse roles and play a 2-octave unison ascending altered dominant scale, six notes and then seven. The G♮ at the start of the 7-note phrase is the lower neighbor to the A♭.

Putting All the Motifs Together

The trumpets then jump up into a syncopated Cmaj7 voiced in Drop 2, which is followed by parallel major 7th chords descending in whole steps very much like the saxes in **Measure 6** of the intro—only this time, rather than being syncopated, the quarters are on the beat—five short and then one long and one short. The long/short quarters are the inversion of our *motif b* from **B1-2**, only extended and combined with our whole-tone movement.

This phrase is echoed by the trombones in descending triads. Although the 1st Trombone continues the trumpet whole step pattern, his first note is the 3rd of an E♭ triad rather than the major 7th that the first trumpet has been playing. The bones end up on a C♭ triad (the tritone sub of the tonic F) over which the piano plays the final 4-note descending diatonic scale. This time it is *fa, mi, re, do—do* being the +11 of the C♭ chord. The bass and drums answer with a final Charleston.

[Now listen again to the entire chart, **3-1: Complete Arrangement**. At the end, do you feel satisfied that the two central motifs (*a* and *b*) were fully explored and developed, so that ultimately we understand how, while they appeared at the outset to be opposites (legato descending 8th notes and long/short ascending quarter notes), they are really two expressions of the same idea?

One last thing to consider: the game of setting up expectations and delivering surprises at the optimal moments. Surprises come in the guise of rhythm, melody, harmony, orchestration, form, phrase lengths, dynamics and articulations. The constants are the steady beat and the sophisticated character of the piece.

I could have said this a hundred times during this analysis, but I saved it until the end: 99% of what I've been talking about was unknown to me while I was writing the chart. In fact, while writing the analysis, I was surprised at these relationships. Basically, I just wrote what sounded good to me. Somewhere in my brain, I was aware of where I was in the song form, and a few of the voicings were tweaked or suggested by my conscious, logical mind, but all the motivic development was completely unknown to me until this moment. I wasn't even aware of the motivic structure of the song until now. I just never thought about it. I let the chart write itself.

Could I have written this chart 50 years ago (before I played in a ton of bands, listened to thousands of recordings, transcribed and studied thousands of classic charts, solos, and recordings? Absolutely not! All that language is stored somewhere in my head and comes out when I speak the language of jazz.]

4. The Rising Storm

[At www.suchsweetthundermusic.com/pages/ cjca-accompanying-files listen to **4-1: Complete Arrangement**. Now ask yourself these three questions that I ask myself whenever I listen to music:

1. What do you like about this chart?
2. What don't you like?
3. How might you do it differently?]

Embracing Two of my Heroes

In my salad days, I dated a young woman who was taking a jazz history course at NYU. Horace Silver was the guest speaker at one class. I accompanied her to this class with the hope of learning how Horace became a great composer. After he spoke a bit, Horace opened the floor to questions, so I asked him, "I get that Bud Powell is your major influence in your piano playing, but who are your compositional influences?" His answer was, "Only one—Duke Ellington." I told him that I was very surprised, because to me their music seemed so different—but he assured me that it was true.

For the next 30 years I still couldn't hear it, until I wrote **The Rising Storm**. The opening section reminds me of Horace, and the middle section bears a great resemblance to the late Ellington suites—specifically **Afro Bossa** and **Far East Suite**. When I finished writing this chart, I understood exactly what Horace meant. There is a core in Ellington's music that Horace picked up on and was able to apply to his bebop aesthetic. If I listen to **The Rising Storm** from one perspective, it is coming right out of Horace Silver, but if I listen to it with Ellington in mind, it fits perfectly into that genre. For me, this piece is very satisfying because it lives on the common ground of two of my favorite composers. I never considered this, but when I hear Isaac play the piano melody on the **A** section it sometimes reminds me of another one of my favorites, Ahmad Jamal. Nothing wrong with that.

Compositional Procedure

When I write arrangements, 99% of the time I go directly to score paper, with no sketches. For original compositions I sometimes go straight to the score paper (*Marlowe, Stompin' On A Riff,* etc.). Sometimes I get an idea and sketch the beginning (in concert pitch) until I know that it is good enough to write a chart. I rarely sketch more than 32 bars.

When I started sketching **The Rising Storm**, the ideas were coming so fast that I didn't want to take the time to go to my closet, get some score paper and transfer what I had sketched. So I just kept on sketching until I got stuck. Except that I never got stuck. The entire piece was written in a few hours—everything except the drums. I copied the parts myself directly from the sketch. I only made a full score years later, in order to apply for a grant.

This is unusual for me. I used the same procedure that Duke Ellington and Billy Strayhorn used: saxes on two staves, brass on two staves. The bones are written stems up and the bass is written on the same bass clef—stems down. When Wynton Marsalis was first starting to arrange, I showed him some of Duke's scores, and he adopted the same system. I prefer to write full transposed scores, but I can understand how concert sketches can be helpful. My teacher, Ray Wright, made concert sketches before writing a transposed full score. I never felt the need to do this. Whatever works for you.

Orchestration Helping to Define the Form

When I set out to write this piece, I was thinking of a feature for our pianist, Isaac ben Ayala. I wanted to give him the melody and then integrate him into the band without losing sight of him being the focal point. The overall form of this multi-themed piece is *ABA*—piano trio/band/piano trio.

Pianist Isaac Ben Ayala.

Each of those big sections has its own song form and can be further broken down into *aba* and a different, but similar, *aaba*. In the secondary theme, the second and third *a* sections start out like the first *a* section but veer into different directions, so I'll notate them with primes. In order to distinguish the two themes, I'll call the *B* section (secondary theme) *cc'dc"*.

The form for the entire piece is: Intro, *aba'* for the *A* section (primary theme) and *cc'dc"* which repeats, then a 16-bar interlude *(e)* and *cc'd* followed by a *DS* back to *aba'* and vamp.

The intro is in C major, the *A* section (primary theme) is in C minor but ultimately cadences in C major. In Baroque and Renaissance music, ending a piece set in minor on a tonic major chord was said to "employ a Picardy third." The *B* section (secondary theme) of the piece is essentially in C major, although the borrowed Fm chords in the bridge *(d)* give us a brief moment of the minor mode. The interlude *(e)* is in Cm and then it's back to C major for the rest of *B* and C minor for the return of *A* (primary theme). The final cadence in major is repeated as a vamp.

Key Signatures

I was, and still am, torn about whether to use a key signature of three flats for the C minor section of this chart. If a bridge to a song modulates to a different key, I don't change key signatures, but this C minor section is 24 bars long—much longer than most bridges. My reasons for not changing key signatures here are:

1. The final cadence is in C major.
2. It's not worth the confusion that key signature changes create for a few notes.
3. We are only changing mode; not key centers.

The Intro

The intro should contain the essential DNA of the entire piece.

In this case the melodic and harmonic motifs of the piece are spelled out in the first measure—the melodic half steps (A# to B) and the minor 3rd, (spelled enharmonically, A# to G), the blue note (the ♭7—A#) juxtaposed with a non-blues major 7th sonority.

Right away this piece reminded me of Max Steiner's beautiful theme from *Adventures in Paradise*, a TV show I used to watch as a kid because I liked the music so much. The show was about a guy who sailed the South Pacific in his yacht. I loved how Steiner's music conjured up the expanse and tranquility of the water.

Getting back to our intro, note how the second measure inverts the minor 3rd interval to a major 6th, then back to the minor 3rd and finally moves up a whole step for the resolution on *la* (the note of wonder). The whole step is a slightly expanded version of our half-step motif. Also notice how the piano left hand moves in minor 3rds and half steps before it arpeggiates the C triad with an added

9th. That arpeggio demonstrates the idea of expansion—first a 5th, then a 6th and finally a 7th.

The chords in the intro were carefully chosen. Although the G melody in measure 1 is the consonant 5th of the tonic Cmaj7, the Bb's in the bar cast a strong blues tinge against the sophisticated major 7th sonority. This discrepancy makes me cringe a bit. It immediately sets up the picture I have in mind for this piece:

We are enjoying a relaxing cruise on a yacht in the magnificently pale blue South Pacific, but danger (an approaching storm) is threatening, and we will need to deal with it. This setting is an obvious metaphor for our seemingly peaceful and secure lives that are more precarious than we'd like to admit.

Sailboat on the Pacific, ©2008 by Jeff Saxsma. Courtesy of the photographer.

The F melody in **measure 2** forms the 9th on the Eb6—a most recognizable and stable pentatonic voicing. The return to the G melody in **measure 3** cries out for something daring. Putting a D7 below it creates a dissonant minor 9th interval between the G and the lower F# and begs for resolution. This wrong-note voicing must be explored later in the piece. The Dbmaj7 in the next bar gives some resolution—the G is the +11, which creates a volatile tritone between the melody and the root. Repeating the G establishes the tonality and says,

"Here comes the tonic." Sure enough, we get a C chord on **measure 5**, but the 6th (connoting awe) is in the melody and the 9th is added in the left hand arpeggio to make it feel slightly out of kilter, but still consonant and relaxing.

Establishing the Tempo

Once the Latin beat establishes the tempo on the resolution in the fifth bar, we stay there for the rest of the piece. I felt that because of the big *ABA* form, we needed a more grandiose intro than I would necessarily use for a simple song form. The same logic would apply to the intro to the first movement of a multi-movement work.

The Primary Theme

The entire *a* section of the piano melody (**A1-8**) consists of minor 6ths, major 6ths and minor 2nds. Although most of my melodies consist mainly of upper partials of the chords 9ths, 11ths and 13ths), the only note above a 7th in these 8 bars is the -9 in **A5**. The wide intervals and colorful harmonic progression create the interest.

The Shoulder Chord

I've always associated the bVI7 with Duke Ellington (*Mood Indigo, I'm Beginning To See The Light, Dusk,* et al) and Johnny Green's great standard, *Out Of Nowhere.* Alexander Courage used it in the *Star Trek Theme* and claimed to have showed the shoulder chord to Green. The shoulder chord? When Courage told the story, he would play the piano, and when he got to the bVI7, he would turn his head to the left, squint and raise his left shoulder.

The Circle of Fifths

Following the shoulder chord, the changes move around the circle of 5ths; E7 A7 D7 G7. In itself this is nothing remarkable, but what makes it interesting is the E7. The E root is the major 3rd in C minor. We expect a diatonic chord like Dm7-5 or G7, or even the tritone sub of G7 (D♭7). E♮ in C minor is the most outlandish note we could use. It's the major 3rd in a minor key. When we are in a major key, we often borrow chords from the minor to add color. The reverse is rare, but here it is.

Add to that, we also have the -9 in the melody. The minor 9th is a tricky interval. As a teenager I was taught to avoid it—and so I did, until I heard it in Ellington's music and became attracted to this taboo sound. I have since come to use it with care. I've already pointed out a few instances in other charts as well as the D11 in the intro to this piece. I will show more examples in this chart as they come up in key places.

What to Tell the Rhythm Section

I'd like the rhythm section to function as a trio, so I'm just giving the piano the melody and chord changes. The bass just needs the pattern in the first bar and chord changes after that. I'd like drums to play with brushes for the primary theme and with sticks on the secondary theme. The switch will help define the form and add to the intimacy of the trio on the top and the end. I'm not specific about what the drums need to play, as long as it has a Latin feel and fits with the piano and bass. Jimmy and I never discussed this. He knew immediately what to do to make this piece sound good.

When you've got good, experienced musicians, you want to get their creative input. Neither Ellington nor Strayhorn wrote drum parts. Wynton Marsalis has followed this tradition. I don't have as much rehearsal time as they did and do, so I provide a guide for the drums. I basically want to let him know what the band is doing, so he can create his own part. Drummers must listen, and then lead the band, while providing the beat, color and continuity. It is essential for everyone in the band to understand the arrangements, but this is crucial for the rhythm section, since, for the most part, we expect them to improvise their parts.

Expanding the Intervals

B1-8 is the *b* section of this theme. It needs to oppose the *a* section. Curiously, I chose to use the same melodic rhythm and shape as the first 4 bars of **A** before going in a different direction for the next four. In fact, the melody is identical for the first six beats of **A** and **B**. After that, I expand all the intervals by a half or whole step, so that instead of 6ths, 3rds and minor 2nds, I now have a minor 7th, 4ths and a major 2nd.

Developing the Harmony

The harmony in this section is developed in two ways. I have sped up the harmonic rhythm, so that it basically moves twice as fast at **B** as it did at letter **A**. This gives the illusion that we are playing a faster tempo. Also, instead of chords with roots that normally resolve down by a 5th and inner voices with 3rds and 7ths that descend by half step, the roots in the first 7 measures form an ascending chromatic scale from C up to B♭ before moving to a more traditional turnaround in C minor: ♭VII ♭III V/V V. In direct contrast to **A**, the melodic pitches venture into more interesting relationships with the bass note (+11, +9, 6th, +5, major 7th, 11th) before the turnaround, which is designed to gently transition back to the theme from **A**.

When I wrote this passage, I heard the melody and then knew that I wanted an ascending bass line. Once that was in place I had two notes in each chord (melody and bass) and easily filled in the other two. Although the initial idea of the ascending bass line came from my subconscious, I used my logical conscious mind to work out all the details. In the end I always ask myself if what I wrote sounds good and feels satisfying. It doesn't matter how hip something looks if it can't pass the Ellington test: If it sounds good, it *is* good.

Harmony is a convention that we use. We tend to think of it as vertical structures, but in reality, harmony is the confluence of melodic lines.

When I was in high school, we played a lot of stock arrangements. These were published arrangements that could be played by a rhythm section and anywhere from one horn up to eleven horns. The idea was that the harmonies would always sound complete. To accomplish this, the arrangers would ignore voice leading and create voicings. I quickly came to understand that stocks were inferior to specials (arrangements written for a certain orchestration). It was apparent that the awkwardness of playing your part left you feeling unsatisfied. I was always told that stocks were a necessary evil, since not every band has the same instrumentation.

As I became more aware of Duke Ellington's music, I noticed that his band always sounded good, even when players were missing. I never noticed that there were important pitches missing in some chords. My buddies and I deduced that it was the strength of the voice leading. Jimmy Hamilton told me this story: After a few days of absence from the band, Paul Gonsalves returned. When a certain harmonized passage came up, Jimmy leaned over and told Paul to *tacet* his part because it sounded better without him! Sometimes less is more.

Completing the Primary Theme

Letter **C** returns to the first 4 bars of **A** before moving into a final surprise cadence in C major. The F on the downbeat of **C5** descends a minor 2nd from Gb in **C4**, and then jumps up a major 6th to D. We have our expansion in (minor 6th to major 6th) reverting back to the original in **C5** (major 6th) before we get a slightly larger expansion of a major 7th (D down to D#) and the final upward minor 2nd (the inversion of the descending major 7th). The D# is an enharmonic spelling of Eb (the minor 3rd of C minor). I chose to use the enharmonic D# to avoid an extra accidental (E♮ in **C7**).

[Listen to **4-2: Intro & 1st Theme (mm 1-D)**. Does the piano trio paint a picture? Is there sufficient rhythmic, melodic, and harmonic interest to offset the lack of instrumental color from the resting horns? Do the unusual chord changes feel natural and inevitable?]

The Secondary Theme (What is This Piece Really About?)

Right from the start, despite its being in C major, the intro to this piece contains numerous Bb's, Eb's, Ab's, and even Db's and a Gb (notated enharmonically as F#). After cadencing in C major, we abruptly shift to C minor on the next measure (**A1**). **A**, **B** and **C** are in C minor until the final cadence in C major. At this point, we have a sudden, unprepared modulation (or more specifically, change of mode) to the parallel major (C major). The next 32 bars are in C major with some blue notes and a few Ab's (the b6th, which is borrowed from the minor mode). The bridge at **F** uses the *ivm* (also borrowed from C minor).

An interesting reversal happens in the interlude at **L** and **M**. The F7 is a *IV* chord in C major with a flatted 7th (E♭ is the 3rd in C minor, but the A♮'s in the F7 chords make us feel like we are still in C major, albeit with a tinge of the blues). The following Cm is clearly a reference to our original Cm theme at letter **A**. After three plagal cadences *(IV i)* in Cm, we go to A7 (the *V/ii* in both C major and minor, but with more allegiance to C major because of the A♮ root), A♭7 (*♭VI* in C minor with a ♭5 blue note) and finally Dm7-5 G7 (*ii V* in C minor). The Cmaj7 on the downbeat of **M1** is a pleasant and somewhat surprising return back to our C major theme.

To sum all this up, for me, this piece is about the shifting of modalities back and forth from major and minor. We feel the brightness and darkness. Add to this, the sensuality of the blues, and how it can inhabit and affect both modalities.

Sameness and Difference

I am always concerned with the opposites of sameness and difference. They are crucial to keeping the audience interested. Too much sameness will produce boredom, and too much difference will lead to confusion and frustration. Somewhere in the middle lies the happy land of delight. Actually, there is quite a bit of leeway. Some artists challenge us more than others.

Moving from One Section of a Piece to Another

How much do we need to change to keep things interesting? How much do we need to retain to achieve continuity and consistency? When there is a major change in groove, melody (introducing a new song in a medley or overture), key or orchestration, we need to retain most of the other elements somewhat, in order not to sound like we just switched

stations on the radio. When we change *two* elements, we need to retain even more.

At letter **D** we make a major change in orchestration—going from piano trio to full big band. We also change mode from C minor to C major. The groove changes slightly. Although the drummer is still playing a Latin groove, he switches from brushes to sticks. Even though this is mostly a change of color, he may also change his rhythms somewhat—especially in supporting the brass figures.

With all these abrupt and obvious changes, we need the rhythmic, melodic and harmonic material to be very similar to the previous section of the piece. Rhythmically, we retain a Latin groove and the Charleston rhythms of the melody. Melodically, we keep developing the 6th and 2nd. Harmonically, we still use major 7th and 6th chords along with dominant 7ths. There are no diminished, and very few minor 7th and half diminished chords in either section.

In terms of root movement, letter **D** is similar to **B** in the ascending chromatic bass line. **E** starts out and ends ascending, but in between has a chromatically descending bass line. Although the bridge at **F** introduces the plagal cadence, it ends with a chromatically descending turnaround. **G** is like **E**, except that it cadences on the tonic.

Schenkerian Analysis

I don't really remember much about Schenkerian analysis, other than that it deals with analyzing melodies by eliminating auxiliary pitches and boiling everything down to the basic melodic movement. Very often there are two complementary lines operating at the same time within one melodic line. Such is the case in letter **D**.

The upper line is *Example 4-1*, shown below. The lower line is *Example 4-2*.

Compare this to letter **A**, where the upper line is a descending chromatic scale starting on E♭ and ending on B, and the bottom line is a descending chromatic scale from G to F.

You could even say that there is a middle line in **D5-8** of an ascending major 2nd from C to D *(Example 4-3)*. I like when the auxiliary pitches have logic and direction.

The orchestration at **D** is harmonized brass vs. unison reeds. The first 5 bars are call-and-response, and in the last 3 measures, the trombone trio provides harmonic pads for the saxes, who combine with the bass to form 5-part harmony.

Uncharacteristically for me, the lead trumpet repeats the sax unison pitch (G). They

are separated by an octave, but even still, they form an agreement that, on the surface, seems out of place at the beginning of a phrase. I'm not exactly sure why this sounds good to me—no other pitch is as satisfying. I suspect that we need the reinforcement to solidify the change in modality to C major.

Three Trombones vs. Four Trombones

When I was coming up, big bands had either three trombones, or four. At one point in the 1950s Ellington's trombone section came to him and said, "Duke, all the other bands are using four trombones now—why can't we add one?" To which the Maestro replied, "Because then it would be too easy for me to write for you." What he meant was that having three instruments express 4-part harmony was more of a challenge than merely assigning four notes to four players.

Example 4-1. The upper line.

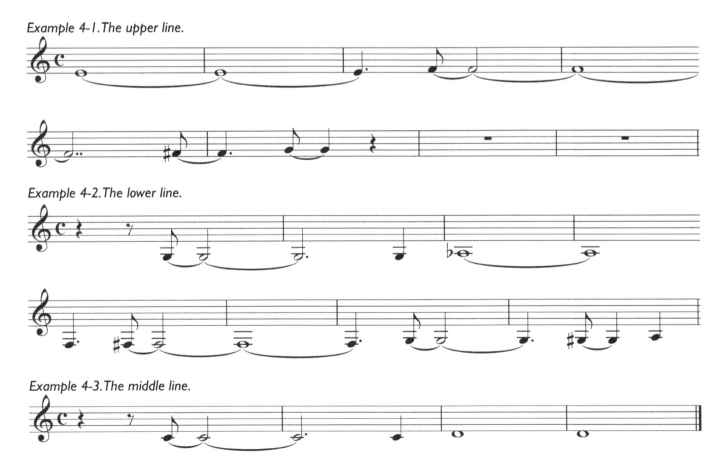

Example 4-2. The lower line.

Example 4-3. The middle line.

In actuality, I find three bones an advantage. For one thing, adding a fourth bone often makes the bones sound too mellow—too syrupy sweet. They lose the bite and the nobility that three have. Also I like to use the trombone section to accompany solo lines and unisons in the saxes and or trumpets. Adding an extra bone makes it harder for the trombone harmonies to avoid the melody notes in the solo or unison line. If one of the bones doubles a melody note, it loses its individuality.

Similarly, when writing for the full brass section, it's hard to find an eighth harmony note. For me, seven is plenty. In most cases, brass sections with more than seven players wind up with a lot of doubling. Even at the octave, I am sensitive about doubling. Sometimes it is desirable, sometimes not.

7-Part Brass Voicings

In most cases, brass section voicings have the bones playing the basic chord tones and the trumpets playing the upper partials. As I've said before, sometimes I like to reverse that relationship. Such is the case in **D1-2**. The trumpets play a close position Cmaj7 while the bones play the 6th, 3rd and 9th. Neither the 6th nor the 9th is included in the trumpet voicing. The 3rd in the 2nd Trombone doubles the 2nd Trumpet at the octave. Normally, we don't double the 3rd in a major chord (unless it is the melody), so why does it sound good here? The traditional reason for not doubling the 3rd is that it can make the chord sound too bright. In this case I want to use the brightness to point out to the listener that we have gone from minor to major.

The trumpets behave similarly in **D4-5**, forming a D♭maj9 (without the root), D♭69 (by just moving the top voice and a D7-9 (again without the root). The bones play D♭ triads

resolving to a Dᵒ. These chords are all voiced tightly, with the 1st Trombone overlapping the 4th Trumpet.

I don't normally overlap, but in this case it sounds good to me. Perhaps it's because of the lead trombone's repeated F's relating obliquely to the 3rd Trumpet's resolution up a half step, which creates a minor 2nd with the trombone. I also like the triads in the bones, which add so much to the noble character of this piece.

Unison Saxes with Trombone Pads

My decision to use rootless voicings in the trombones in **D6-8** was made easy by the range of the tenor trombone. Since low E is its bottom limit, an E♭ root in the trombone is out of the question. (We don't use a bass trombone, or trombones with triggers in my band. We like peashooters, so that the bones can match the trumpets' brightness and not get lost in the ensemble).

The succeeding chords follow suit, even though the roots could be played by the bottom trombone. I like the continuity of the chromatically ascending chords—the bottom two bones move up parallel to the bass, while the 1st Trombone and the saxes skip around in more interesting melodic shapes. The juxtaposition of these two shapes sounds quite complex and sophisticated.

Melody Construction

The C major melody (**D** through **G**) is more similar to the previous C minor melody (**A** through **C**) than it is different; the prevalence of 6th and minor 2nd intervals, the Charleston rhythms and the frugal use of chromatics. This secondary theme is 32 bars long, and uses only a total of eleven notes outside the C major scale (four A♭'s and seven F#'s; with no

Db's, Eb's or Bb's). The limitations and repetitions help to create the character.

Repeating the Texture with Different Pitches and Rhythms

Letter **E** is a slight development of the saxophone melody of **D**. The brass performs the same functions (call-and-response followed by trombone pads). The brass responses reverse the pattern from **E**; multiple jabs, and then a single jab. The trumpets are voiced higher but still consist of 4-part close voicings. The 1st and 3rd Trombones play notes not covered by the trumpets, while the 2nd Trombone doubles the 5th of both chords—5ths are neutral sounding. We have established the major tonality, so doubling the 3rd would sound too bright now.

Octave Doubling Within Voicings

I don't have any rules on what notes to double. I just choose what sounds good to me, based on the sonorities of the brass section, as well as linear considerations for each individual part and its intervallic relationships with the other parts. I think about dissonance and consonance. Are there half steps or tritones, and if so, where do they fall? Which parts rub against which other parts?

In the Cmaj7 voicing in **E1-2**, the only prime dissonance is the major 7th between the 1st and 4th Trumpet. A more usual voicing would be to give the 9th to the 4th Trumpet and the root to the 3rd Trombone on the bottom of the voicing—but this voicing continues the pattern of giving the basic chord sounds to the trumpets on the top of the voicing and the tensions below to the trombones.

The Cmaj9 voicing has a stable sound as opposed to the Db13+11 voicing in **E4**, where there are half steps between the 4th Trumpet

and 1st Trombone as well as between the 2nd and 3rd Trombones. The minor 9th interval between the 1st Trumpet and the 3rd Trombone is tempered by the octave doubling of the Ab in the 1st Trumpet and 2nd Trombone. Had I not doubled the Ab in the trombone, the minor 9th would have dominated the sound, rather than the half step between the two bones.

Developing the Charleston Rhythm

Aside from the melodic use of the Charleston, the bass pattern is made up of a Charleston plus a quarter note on beat 4. This pattern repeats throughout the piece. (I suspect that the pattern originated in the Middle East, and spread across North Africa with the Moors and into pre-Inquisition Spain. Then, starting in 1492, it crossed the Atlantic Ocean to South America, Central America, and the Caribbean Islands before arriving in New Orleans. From New Orleans it spread into jazz and popular music in the 20th century.) In **E5-6** the bones join the bass in this rhythm, which is a development of what the bones played in **D7-8**.

Call-and-response

When the saxes come to rest on the tonic in **E7-8**, the bones respond actively with a descending and then ascending chromatic figure, rather than merely supplying a passive pad. Instead of having the bass agree with the sax tonic, I used a deceptive cadence, so that the C tonic pitch becomes the 3rd of an Ab6 chord. The bones start with a Drop 2 voicing of Ab6 minus the C, which is played by the saxes. The following bone voicings are merely chromatic. Each voicing relates in a different way to the C in the saxes and the bass line. It looks a lot wilder than it sounds. We understand the Ab tonality and just experience the trombone movement as colorful chromatic filigree.

Contraction and Expansion

Letter **F** is the bridge of the secondary theme, so it needs to feel opposite in nature to the *a* sections of this essentially *aaba* form. Starting with the three pickups to **F**, the orchestration reverses, so that the brass takes over the melody with an answer from the saxes in **F3**. We are expecting a descending major 6th in **F1**, since that is how the previous two 8-bar phrases started. We get a descending wide interval, but it is a perfect 5th, a whole step short of a major 6th.

This phrase being opposite to the *a* section, the third and fourth bars descend rather than ascend. The descent is a minor 7th, a half step larger than the major 6th motif of the *a* section. So we have a slightly smaller interval and a slightly larger interval. The syncopated rhythm of **F1** and **F3** is also an expansion of the Charleston rhythm of **D1** and **E1**.

The Chord of Despair

As I've said before, every note in the scale and every chord evokes an emotional response in the listener. The last 500 years of Western music have conditioned us in a Pavlovian way. I don't know if it is universal to humans (and possibly animals and plants—I suspect it may be), but people who have grown up listening to Western music have very similar associations.

(I'm not really kidding about plants. There have been studies with plants that prove that they grow better when exposed to classical music or jazz. I know this is purely anecdotal, but a long time ago a saxophone player buddy of mine had a plant in his living room that committed suicide. One day my friend came home and found the plant on the floor instead of in its pot on the table. I know you are thinking that the cat must have done it, but my friend lived alone and didn't have any pets. A puzzlement, to be sure!)

But I digress. Each chord has its emotional baggage. The *iv* minor is the chord of despair. There is no sadder chord in all of music. We can soften it by adding a minor 7th, or make it truly distressing by adding a 6th. Adding the major 7th is not as awful as the 6th, since it doesn't contain the interval of the devil (the tritone).

The tritone between the 3rd and the 6th of a minor 6th chord creates instability in addition to sadness. Adding a 9th gives some tension in conjunction with the 3rd (after all they are a half step apart), but it's more of a distraction than a solution to a more serious problem. If you have any doubts about my sincerity, I suggest that you play through a half dozen standards and check out the lyrics when you get to the *ivm*. This is no joke.

Tranquility and Turbulence

Listen to letters **E** and **F**. We are sailing along nicely, and then there is a little turbulence in **E5-6**, and something is definitely up in **E7-8**. The brass pickups to **F** are a clap of thunder ushering in a black sky and sudden downpour, but quickly the sun comes out with the Cmaj chord in **F3**. The Fm chord in **F5-6** is not so threatening, since the last Fm didn't last long. The turnaround in **F7-8** transitions us right back to calm seas and smooth sailing.

The Fm chord at letter **F** doesn't come out of nowhere. The A♭ deceptive cadence prepares us in a gentle way. The C7♯9 brass pickups make a startling but smooth transition. When we hear that Fm at **F1**, we are not really surprised because there have been so many A♭'s littered throughout the piece. It's only natural that we explore the meaning of A♭ in the key of C.

Trombones Above Trumpets

When I was a kid, I read an interview with Charlie Parker. He was asked if he ever did any arranging. He said that he had some ideas, but he would always wind up with the trombones above the trumpets. Even at a tender age, I realized that this conflicted with the order of the universe. Nevertheless, there have been moments when it occurs to some degree and makes sense.

One such moment happens in **E8-F1**. The diminished triad in the bones resolves to the Fm triad with such majesty. No trumpet can compare. Not only is the lead trombone above the 4th Trumpet for these two voicings, but the 2nd Trombone starts a half step above the 4th Trumpet before resolving in contrary motion. When I used to play trumpet, I didn't like how it felt when the trombones doubled me at the unison, and I certainly didn't like when they were voiced above me, but this is a special moment that feels right due to the contrary motion, unusual spacing and the integrity of the trombone section voicings.

The Sun Comes Out

The Cmaj9 voicing in **F3** is the same voicing as the brass chord in **D1-2**, with its 3rd doubled at the octave for brightness, and its 9th on the bottom for the irritating feeling of a pebble in your shoe. Rather than repeating this C chord on the *and* of beat 4, I went to a C7, which is the dominant of Fm (the next chord) and, since we are going to Fm, I added a -9 to the C7. However, the melody note in the 1st Trumpet is an A♮, which clearly keeps us in F major.

The trumpets jump down to a C13-9 in close position, while the bones play the 5th, root and ♭5 on the bottom. I like the instability and

dissonance that the ♭5 creates on the bottom of the voicing.

While all this is going on, the unison saxes play a blues scale lick that includes the ♭7, ♭5 and 4 before hitting the ♭3 with the brass on the *and* of beat 4. Although it is a bit unusual to use these blue notes on a major 7th chord, I established a blues context earlier, so we "buy" it.

Tutti Voicings

The horns all come together in **F5-6** for 2 bars of *tutti* voicings played with long quarter notes. The long and smooth notes in this piece provide the prevailing calmness of the warm water and gentle breeze in our sails, while the short quarters and 8th notes signify turbulence. The 2nd Trumpet is *tacet* for 4 bars, so that he can prepare for his plunger solo at **G**. The top four brass (three trumpets plus one trombone) are voiced in 4-part close harmony. The bottom two bones double the top two trumpets down the octave, and the saxes double the brass at the unison, starting with the 2nd Trumpet. I have given the bottom tenor rest, so that the bari will double the lead trumpet down the octave.

Rather than voice all eight notes with static Fm6 voicings, I alternated Fm6 with C7-9 voicings. The final C on the *and* of beat 4 of measure **F6** is the climax of this section (and the highest note of the entire chart). This deserves something special to set it off from the rest. I have the trumpets play in octaves (one up and three down), *tacet* the bones (so they will sound fresh with their answers at **G**) and have given the saxes chromatically descending +9 chords voiced in open position with the powerful root/5th on the bottom.

Note that the 4th Tenor is in his extreme low register, and will need to use subtone in order to blend with the other saxes. I suppose I could have continued the chromatic descent one more chord from the D7+9 to a D♭7+9, but the plain G7 is perfectly satisfying in this spot.

When the simple solution works, I prefer it to something more complex.

Individual Instrumental Tonal Considerations

The unusual doubling of the altos on the final note of **F8** is the result of contrary motion. I was only hearing four pitches in that chord. Doubling at the octave or adding an additional note destroyed the directness of this dominant chord. Another option would have been to double the tenors rather than the altos. I'm not sure what my thinking was at the time, but most likely, I was hearing the sounds of the individual players in my mind.

I don't recall who told me this story—possibly Al Murray, who was there. At an Ellington rehearsal in the 1950s, the band was reading down a new Billy Strayhorn chart, which sounded phenomenal. Duke asked, "Billy, would you mind if I try something?" To which Billy responded, "Sure, Duke." Ellington instructed two of the trombonists to switch their notes in a particular ensemble voicing, "Britt, you play Butter's note, and Butter, you play Britt's note." Then he had the entire band play that voicing with the change.

Although the voicing had the identical pitches and instrumentation, the subtle change in timbre made it sound like an entirely different chord. When Duke wanted to lay a compliment on someone, he liked to say that they were "beyond category," but Ellington's ear and knowledge of timbre were not only beyond category, they were beyond perfect pitch.

[Now listen to **4-3: Secondary Theme (D-H)**. Is it satisfying in being the opposite and yet the same as the primary theme (**A** through **C**)? Does it tell a compelling story? Do we want to hear more development?]

Solos

Scoring Solos

Although the character of many of the great big bands of the past was built around the leader's instrumental sound playing the melody of songs, modern bands rarely have written passages for solo instruments. Melodies of jazz tunes are generally scored as unison or harmonized passages. Solos are generally improvised; the Ellington band was the most notable exception. There were a number of distinct personalities on different instruments who were often given melodies to play.

At **G** I gave Fletch an 8-bar written trumpet solo (the melody) to be played with a plunger. To make it sound nasty, I had him insert a pixie mute (they used to be called plugs or French straight mutes back in the day) under the plunger. This solo needs to be a sudden shift away from the peacefulness of the previous piano solo. I added the adjective "Nasty" to the trumpet part, just to be clear.

Contrasting Personalities

Letter **G** contrasts three uniquely different sounds and emotions. The trumpet is pinched and nasty. The unison saxes ornament the major 7th of the C chord before ornamenting the 6th of the D♭ chord. Note the half-step relationship between these two pitches, as well as the half steps that make up the ornaments.

The trombones play the noble hero slaying the fire-breathing trumpet dragon, while the saxophones' maiden looks passively on—paralyzed with fear, but not showing any emotion. Although the bones are merely echoing the trumpet in the first phrase, their triads signal their nobility, while their half step planing ties them to the saxes.

Since the trumpet has the 3rd of the D♭ chord in **G3-4**, I omitted that note from the bones and gave them a D♭maj7 voicing that alternates with a Dmaj7, and finishes on a G major triad (the tritone sub of D♭). A half beat later, the rhythm section plays a D♭7 with the saxes descending from the 5th to the 9th. D♭7 is the dominant of the upcoming G♭ chord. The triadic bones merely move chromatically from G to G♭.

The saxes *tacet* the next 2 bars before they return with a chromatically ornamented 6th on the final tonic of this chorus. Notice how this figure is identical in rhythm and ornamentation to **G1-2**, but uses the 6th (like **G3-4**) instead of the major 7th of **G1-2**.

Combining different ideas like this unifies the piece and satisfies our need for resolution.

In **G5-6** the bones act in concert with the bass, while the solo trumpet plays slightly different rhythms to assert his individuality. The 4- and 5-part harmony created in these two measures is complex in the way it fights the natural urge to move all the voicings parallel with the chromatically descending bass. The trumpet cadences on the 9th of the tonic, answered by the saxes on the 6th (our "happy" note) and finally, by the majestic trombones, who extend their chromatic approach to include the lower as well as the upper neighbor triad (C, B, C, D♭ and C) before firmly establishing the tonality for the piano solo with a unison 5, 1 period.

Choosing Soloists

Assigning solos comes down to two considerations: instrumentation and personality.

Instrumentation

Piano solos: Each instrument functions differently in the ensemble. Piano solo intros are often used as musical count-offs in the tradition of Count Basie and Duke Ellington. These can be two, four, six, or eight bars, and often are a 32-bar chorus or one or more choruses of blues. Such is the case in *Stompin' On A Riff*. A written band intro can precede or follow the piano solo. This happens in *Do It Again*.

Piano solos often serve as palate cleansers between "courses." For instance, in the solo section of a chart following the last horn solo, the piano calms things down before they heat up again in the shout chorus. Listen to *Bumper Cars* on my **Hindustan** CD. Similarly the piano can solo (usually briefly) between the shout and the recap or, if there is no recap, between the shout and the coda.

Sometimes the piano can be used for vamp endings (usually in conjunction with a fade). Such is the case in my chart of *On The Atchison, Topeka And The Santa Fe* from my octet CD, **I Had The Craziest Dream**. In this case it was only natural to give the ending vamp to the piano, since this is a piano feature number—the pianist plays the intro, solos on the bridge of the head, and is the only soloist in the solo section.

Of course the piano can be a soloist in the solo section of a chart. The piano does not have the power of a horn, so I almost never write backgrounds behind a piano solo, lest the pianist be overpowered and seem weak. However, the piano can hold his own in call-and-response patterns with the horns, as evidenced briefly in the shout chorus of the aforementioned *Bumper Cars*.

Bass solos: The acoustic string bass is rather soft and delicate, so if there are any backgrounds during a bass solo, they must be quite soft and written above the bass tessitura. Bass solos and drum solos differ from solos by other instruments. When the bass or drums solo, they cease playing their *continuo* function (a major part of the groove). This change in groove must be considered—in the right place it can be a major asset.

Bass solos occur with the least frequency of the instruments commonly used in jazz. Mike Richmond once told me that, in the ten months he played bass in Horace Silver's quintet, he played exactly two solos. This is also the case in big band writing. Bass solos were extremely rare during the Swing Era, which made Jimmy Blanton's recordings with Ellington in 1940 groundbreaking. If you are looking for a change of pace, consider a bass solo.

Check out Dennis Irwin's bass solo on *No Refill* (**Hindustan** CD). Dennis's follows the piano solo in the tradition of most small group jazz. In the three *a* sections of the tune he is accompanied by only the piano and drums. The bridge has soft horn backgrounds, ending with two emphatic exclamation points from the bones.

Over the last 40 years I have worked quite a bit with bassist Chuck Israels. I've noticed that when he plays a solo, he always rests for the first bar or two before starting to solo. I mentioned this to him recently, and he told me that, when an instrument moves from the background to the foreground, the listener needs a moment to readjust. Sometimes there is a high and loud ensemble figure just prior to a bass solo (as in Thad Jones' *Three And One*). The bass tacets the ensemble figure, which ends in a fall-off and space for the bass.

Drum solos are rarely accompanied. They are sometimes interspersed with horn figures in call-and-response. Drum solos are generally short—four or eight bars. It's nice, maybe once a night, to let the drummer stretch out. He can solo on the form of the piece, or freely (usually out of tempo). Sometimes drummers will intuitively solo in the context of your piece. Other times you may need to encourage them.

Drum solos are generally loud and exciting, but they can also be soft and subtle (especially when played with brushes) and everything in between. One of my all-time favorite drum solos is *40 Lashes* from Wynton Marsalis' **Blood On The Fields**. Herlin Riley applies a beating we will never forget. This is programmatic music at its best—the music serves the story.

Choosing Which Horn to Solo

Change of color from the passage preceding the solo and the passage following the solo—it's usually best to think in terms of opposites. Ellington's general rule was that a horn soloist should have at least 8 bars' rest before and after his solo, so that he can move to and from the microphone or just have time to focus and refocus.

Another important consideration is the orchestration of the background figures. Again the principle of opposites applies. Brass solos are accompanied by reed backgrounds and vice versa. This doesn't always apply (as we heard in *Hindustan* when the brass accompanied the trombone solo), but it's a good general concept that works more than 90% of the time. Don Redman established this convention in his charts for Fletcher Henderson's band nearly a century ago, and it still makes sense—it helps the listener distinguish between the soloist and the accompaniment (foreground and background).

Individual Personalities in the Band

Say you want an alto sax solo, and you have two alto players in your band. Which one do you give the solo to? I think about whose musical personality best fits this piece, and the particular section of the piece. I also try to spread the solos around, so that everyone gets a chance to play, and when they do, it's something that they will sound good on.

The Solo Section

Having completed a 32-bar *aaba* chorus, at **H** we now embark on the second chorus, which is generally given to soloists. Since this is a piano feature piece, I give the piano a half chorus (16 bars) to improvise.

The trumpet returns at **J** to play the bridge with 5-part sax figures behind him for 4 bars that begin and end with root position spread chords. The three C7 voicings are based on the diminished scale and have the 3rd, -9 and 5th on the bottom. Starting at **J**, the voicings are built in 5ths and then revert to 4ths (perfect and diminished) and finally a 4-part close voicing over the root. The saxes then lay out for 4 bars (**J5-8**), so that the baritone solo at **K** is a fresh color.

Another Written Solo

The baritone plays the "heroic" melody at **K**. Carl is free to add personality, much as Fletch did earlier, except that Fletch played the dragon, while Carl is the heroic knight who has come to slay the dragon.

Compound Voicings

The trombone answers to the bari solo are somewhat unique. If you consider the held note in the baritone sax to be the lead note of the bone answer, and then voice the trombones downward in 4-part close harmony, you get a Cmaj7. The bones then move up and down chromatically, much as they have before in this piece. The baritone's G, which was the 5th of the Cmaj7, now becomes the -5 of the D♭ sandwich chords. In the following response in **K3-4**, the bones enter a beat earlier and fill out a D♭maj7, but instead of planing to a Dmaj7, they move in contrary motion to a G triad (the F in the baritone makes the 7th), which is the tritone sub of D♭. The same thing happened a chorus earlier in **G4**. The baritone then continues with just the rhythm section for two bars.

Omitting the bones once again clears our palate, so that we can be shocked by the brass chord at **K7**. The two bars of rest for the bones in **K5-6** also give the top two bones time to remove their plungers and place them on their music stands. The brass sting in **K7-8** is a C7 with alterations from the diminished scale. The brass is voiced in a symmetrical fashion. Both the top three voices and the bottom three voices consist of a tritone and a perfect 4th. This dramatic punctuation sets up a major change in orchestration, texture, melody, rhythm and form.

The Interlude

Interludes are passages between the parts of a song or arrangement. They give us a relief from the prevailing form. You could say that they function in music much as vacations do in our lives.

When you are on vacation, you don't have the structure of your regular job, but you are aware that you will return to work when the vacation is over. On vacation, you may do things that you can't do the rest of the year, but you are still you. For me a fulfilling vacation is as different from my daily routine as possible. Staying home and not working doesn't feel like a vacation to me.

I live in New York City. I write and perform music. Every day I read the newspaper, watch some TV, and tend to my business dealings. I don't want to do any of these things when I'm on vacation.

I want to go to Italy, try to speak and understand Italian, discover new restaurants and foods I can't get at home, see art and architecture and beautiful scenery, meet people who have a different culture, and see life differently from the way I do in New York.

Even though I'm thousands of miles from home, I'm still going to be me. I'm not going to change my name or how I look, nor will I feel or behave in ways that are much different than usual—a bit more relaxed, but still me.

Or I might vacation somewhere with warm weather, sun and a beach. I'll bring my swimming trunks that don't get used at home. Of course, I will still do *some* of the things that I do at home, like breathing, sleeping, eating, learning, interacting with other people, finding humor, and playing tennis.

When I get home from a vacation, I feel refreshed and eager to get back to the form and trappings of my usual life. Some vacations are only for a weekend. Some are longer. I used to go to Martha's Vineyard for three months at a time when I was a young man, but I always knew that I would return to New York on Labor Day.

Sameness and Difference

Musical interludes should seem as different from the rest of the piece as possible without losing the core personality of the piece. The superficial elements should sound different, but underneath, the same motifs and structures are at work—they are just organized in a new way.

Formal Considerations

The form of the interlude must differ greatly from the surrounding sections. Since we are in a 32-bar *aaba* form, our interlude should be neither 32-bars nor *aaba*. Letters **L** through **M** are 16 measures, consisting of four 4-measure phrases. The first three phrases are nearly identical—only the last note of the middle phrase is different. The fourth phrase is the same for seven beats and then cadences on a G double whole note.

Rhythm

Although our theme (**D** through **G**) consists of 4-bar phrases, the repetition happens after 8 bars and is not verbatim. Melodically the theme uses mostly dotted half notes and syncopations, which create a relaxed feeling. Conversely, the interlude is all 8th notes and 8th note triplets, so it feels almost like it is moving three times as fast as the theme. The only syncopation occurs on the *and* of beat 1 in **L3**, **L7** and **M3**. The overall feeling in the interlude is agitation. The plunger muted trombone responses are even more intensely agitated.

Texture

The texture of the interlude is unison cross-sectional writing (saxes and bones) as opposed to the mostly harmonized sectional writing in the rest of the chart. The call-and-response in the interlude is very cut and dried, as opposed to the more subtle approach to the counterpoint in the theme.

Modality

Our theme is in C major, while the interlude is in C minor, which refers back to the piano theme at the start of the piece. The chord progression of the bridge of the theme is essentially Fm to C and repeat, while the interlude reverses the major and minor relationships by going from F7 to Cm. While both the bridge and the interlude end with turnarounds that will take us back to C major, the progressions are vastly different: A7 A♭7 Dm7-5 G7 over four bars and E7 E♭7 D7 G7 over two bars. Harmonic rhythm is a subtle component that affects listeners greatly.

Common Core

So with all these differences, what—besides our reversal of major and minor, the same key center (C), and the constant tempo and groove—is the underlying core that remains common to the theme and the interlude?

Throughout the piece the predominance of blue notes gives us a blues tinge. The melody of the interlude is out-and-out blues scale (C, E♭, F, F# and G). The crucial idea is the conflict of F# and G, with G winning out in the end and holding it out for two measures—like a celebrating wide receiver dancing in the end zone.

Although the melodic shape is more complicated in our theme, it too centers around the F# to G conflict. Granted, this is some pretty subtle and sophisticated stuff, but that's what makes this interlude so successful. On the surface our vacation bears little relationship to our everyday life, but it sure is fun being

there, and afterwards, it is equally wonderful to settle into the comforts of home again.

Although I like interludes, and they are fun to write, I don't use them all that often. On my **Hindustan** CD, out of 13 charts, only **The Rising Storm** and *The Very Thought Of You* have interludes. Interludes can be useful in any style.

The Soft Shout

An abrupt change of texture and tone. Much of the time, arrangers spend our time creating smooth transitions, but every now and then it is just as important to shock the listener with startling new sounds that are unprepared.

Upper-structure Triads

Letter **M** abruptly changes gears from the interlude. Three saxophone players switch to clarinets to play a paraphrase of the melody that, after the obvious long note, utilizes the quarter note and Charleston syncopations all voiced in triads. The chromatic planing in **M3-4** (back and forth between D♭maj7 and Cmaj7) was foreshadowed in the trombone triads in **G1-2** and **G8** and the chromatic motion in **G4** and **K1-4**.

Aside from the tone color of the instruments and the higher octave, there is a difference in the softness of timbre of the clarinets. Where the bones played noble major triads, the clarinets play minor triads above major chords; Em/C, Fm/D♭, Am/D7, Cm/E♭ and Gm/E♭. Only the F#°/D7 momentarily breaks this pattern.

More 2nds and Minor 3rds

The four unison trumpets play in counterpoint to the clarinets. Their rhythms oppose the clarinet rhythms in such a way that we can hear and understand both lines at the same time. To help us further, the trumpets are an octave below the top clarinet and enlist the use of derbies (also called "hats"). Most bands stopped using derbies 50 years ago, but I still love their sound. They can be fanned to create doo-wahs or kept still to give the illusion of distance, which is what happens here. The clarinets are in the foreground with the trumpets sounding far away in the background.

Like the clarinets, the trumpets move stepwise or by minor 3rds (the inversion of the major 6th interval), except that the order and proportion is reversed. An interesting relationship occurs in the turnaround in **M7-8**. The trumpets continue their line (mimicking what they played in **M3-4**, but the clarinets are replaced by our noble trombones in root position chromatically ascending open triads.

The tenor sax plays a gently ascending line consisting of 7ths and a 6th of the chords, along with the trombone half notes. At the same time, the trumpets play their snaky quarter note line that moves through the upper partials of the chords, and finally lands on the root of the G7 in agreement with the bass and 3rd Trombone. The switch from clarinets to trombones, syncopations to half notes and doubling the harmonic rhythm all build to a climax.

Surprise!

Most musical surprises involve loud and high, and at **N** we are expecting just that. Instead, everyone drops out for a couple of call-and-responses between the bass and the soft *tutti* playing the Charleston rhythm and displaced Charleston. Since the rhythm and the shape of these two *tutti* responses are so recognizable,

I can change the intervals from our motif. Instead of 6ths, I've used a 5th and a 2nd.

The major 7ths in the lead voice keep the tone of the previous passage only to be disturbed by the D♭13-9 in **N3-4**. I have hinted at this dominant of the upcoming G♭ in previous choruses by using the D♭7 for a beat. In **N3-4** it gets a whole measure while the bass finishes his solo. The surprise of the D♭13-9 sets in motion the build to the climax in **N5-8**.

Inverted Tonic Pedal Point vs. Expansion and Contraction

While the trumpets hold their tonic pedal (since their note is on the top, we call it inverted; generally pedals are on the bottom, but they can just as easily be on top or in the middle), the saxes unite with the bass to play 5-part voicings that use contrary motion to expand and then contract.

Notice how, for the first five chords, the bottom three saxes play chromatically descending major triads, and the two altos play the upper parts of the chords which peak on the E♭7 with the lead alto on the natural 11th (I promised there would be some minor 9th intervals—the reason it sounds so good is the contrary motion).

When they get to the A♭7, the lead alto takes over the C from the trumpets. While the saxes hold an A♭9, the bones play an ornamental F (the 13th of A♭7). The saxes and bones hold out their notes for a few beats to build tension before taking a breath for the climax. I used an A♭ dominant chord here instead of the tonic A♭ that appears earlier. This further develops the blues content of the chart, not just with the dominant 7th sonority, but because this G♭ is a blue note along with the E♭ and the B♭.

The Loud Shout

Letter **O** is the shout. It's where everything in this piece comes together and then climaxes in **O8**. The first three notes of the lead trumpet melody in **N8-O1** are the retrograde of the lead alto's last three notes prior to that (**N6-7**). It's our old friend, the combination of the minor 3rd and major 2nd—the essence of the F blues pentatonic. This relationship permeates the unison figures in letter **O**. **O2** adds a major 2nd, **O6** is the same figure transposed up a 4th with the exception of adding the B and C (in the trumpets). The C is another minor 3rd, and the B is the lower neighbor to the C.

The unison trombone figure in **O7-8** is a C blues scale with the exception of the E♮ in **O8**, which is the lower neighbor to the F that follows it, but more importantly it is the half step transposition of the first three notes of the previous measure.

The G♭ blue note is the major 7th on the G7-9+5. The fact that it is a blue note in addition to the intervallic structure justifies the extreme dissonance. Also the G♭ reminds us of the enharmonic F#'s in the fifth and sixth bars of **D**, **E**, and **G**. My band has played this chart at least 100 times, and no one in the band or audience has ever asked me if this is a wrong note. It's quite dissonant, but definitely not wrong.

Full Ensemble Voicings

N8, **O1** and **O5** contain the only full ensemble voicings in the entire piece. The saxes are voiced on the bottom in spread chords, and the bones and trumpets are voiced tightly, with the bones just below the trumpets. This puts the brass in a powerful and bright register.

The Climax

The climax of this piece is the G♭ in the trombones on the *and* of beat 2 in **O8**. It is the peak of the ascending trombone line and creates a wild dissonance with the sax voicing. In addition, the unison trumpets are ascending by 4ths at a much slower pace.

The saxes play a displaced Charleston in **O7** followed by a Charleston in **O8**. Their first three voicings are standard +9 voicings in open position moving chromatically downward. The last voicing condenses into a 4-part close voicing with the root added below.

Returning to the Primary Theme

Although letter **O** is the bridge, when we get to the last measure, it feels like we need to return to our primary theme in the piano, rather than finish out the chorus. This elision gives us some nice forward motion. On the *DS*, letters **A**, **B**, and **C** are repeated and end in a vamp (Cmaj7 to D♭7) that conveys the feeling and mood of this entire piece. The major/minor conflict is played out in the E/E♭ melody. Originally, I was going to do a board fade, but Roger Rhodes, our record producer, talked me out of it. I'm still not sure which way to go. Both endings work for me.

[Let's listen again to **4-1: Complete Arrangement**. Does it feel unified? Are there enough surprises? I didn't set out to do much in this piece, but upon scrutiny, I think there is a lot more going on than one notices at first.]

Coda

Before I leave you, I want to reiterate a few concepts that permeate this book:

1. **Use opposite elements to define form.** The greater the opposites, the more vivid your piece, and the more likely that it will have the potential to be excellent.

2. **Integrate the superficial and the subtle.** Neither can be successful on its own.

3. **Don't underestimate the power of the personal and the impersonal— the individual and the group.** We are each our own person as well as a member of society. We need to experience both to be fully functioning beings. Our music must reflect this.

I encourage you to listen to and study scores of your favorite arrangers and composers. Aim high with your choices. Analyze the music in the same or greater depth as we have in the chapters of this book.

I am currently writing **Creative Composing and Arranging Volume 2**, which will explore songwriting and arranging vocal charts. When I was a young man, I got a call one Friday afternoon from Al Cohn, who was in the midst of orchestrating *Sophisticated Ladies*, which was to open on Broadway on Monday— three days away. The show had been dying in Philadelphia, and a pile of changes and new charts were needed immediately. I hustled to the copyist's office, where I met Al. He was surprisingly relaxed and jovial considering the deadline, but that was Al. He then handed me a few lead sheets and gave me the copyist's phone number.

I naively asked if he had any instructions, to which he said, "It's a vocal chart. It's not a band chart. You know what to do." **Volume 2** will examine what went unsaid that day, and more.

If you have any questions or comments, or want to contact me to buy charts, take lessons, have my band perform, or have me conduct your band, etc., I can be reached at **information@davidbergerjazz.com**.

I wish you many hours of happy writing and listening to your creations. I hope that I have been helpful, answered some of your questions, and gotten you to think about some musical and artistic considerations that you hadn't yet thought of. I have found that the deeper my understanding, the more creative I can be. I hope this works for you as well.

Ever onward and upward,

David Berger
October 16, 2015

Glossary

4-part close harmony (Also called *4-way close* or *block chords*): Voicings with four different pitches within the same octave, and containing a root, 3rd, 5th and 7th (or variations of those pitches).

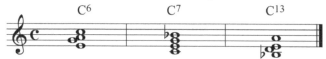

blue note: Notes from the blues scale that are approximately built on the ♭3, ♭5 and ♭7 of the home key. Jazz musicians will color these notes using bends and special intonation to evoke the feeling of the blues.

break: Within the context of an ongoing time feel, the rhythm section stops for one, two, four or even 8 bars. Most often a soloist will improvise during a break.

call-and-response: Repetitive pattern of exchanges either between sections or between ensemble and soloist.

Charleston: The following rhythm:

chart: Arrangement or orchestration.

chromatic: Moving by successive half steps. It can also mean non-diatonic.

coda: (Sometimes called the *outro*) A new section added to create a satisfying ending.

comp: To improvise accompaniment. Short for "accompany."

come sopra: As above.

concerto: Loosely, a piece that features a solo instrument. Traditionally concerti are three movements in length; the first movement being in sonata allegro form. Ellington's concerti *(Concerto For Cootie, Echoes Of Harlem, Boy Meets Horn)* are 1-movement sonata allegro forms, as is Strayhorn's *Charpoy*.

concerto grosso: A piece that features a small group of solo instruments within a larger ensemble. Ellington's *Jam-A-Ditty, Battle Of Swing* and *Launching Pad* are great examples.

constant structure: Transposing a voicing to follow the melody.

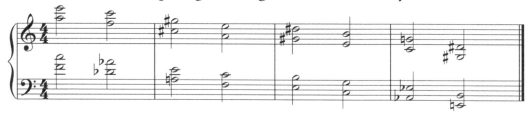

continuo: Improvised Baroque keyboard accompaniment that combines bass notes and chords.

contrary motion: Two or more voices moving in the opposite direction.

cross-sectional orchestration: Scoring for dissimilar instruments in unison or harmony, i.e. trumpet/tenor sax.

derby or hat: Metal mute for brass instruments in the shape of a derby. It may be fanned open and closed, or held still in front of the bell of the instrument, creating a distant sound.

diatonic chords: Those triads and 7th chords that occur naturally (with no accidentals) in major and minor keys. In jazz, although we use all seven chords and call them by number (*I, ii, iii*, etc), we normally only use the formal names for the tonic, dominant and subdominant (*I, IV* and *V*). Also in jazz, very often triads and 7th chords are interchangeable. The chord symbol "C" usually infers that we could add a 6th or a major 7th to the triad.

displaced rhythm: Starting a rhythm on a different beat or part of the beat.

dogfight: A back and forth quick call-and-response where both parts play the same repeated figure, usually separated by an octave and played by different instruments, as in Sousa's *The Stars And Stripes Forever*.

doit: An upward gliss (non-fingered portamento).

Drop 2: Semi-open voicings that are created by taking a 4-part close harmony and dropping the second voice from the top by one octave.

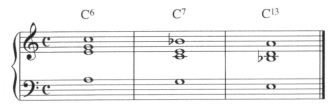

Drop 2 and 4: Semi-open voicings that are created by taking a 4-part close harmony and dropping the second and fourth voice from the top by one octave.

Drop 3: Semi-open voicings that are created by taking a 4-part close harmony and dropping the third voice from the top by one octave.

elision: Omitting the end of a phrase, so that the next phrase begins early.

fall-off: A downward non-fingered portamento. Fall-offs can be very short (also known as a Snooky Young fall-off—generally a half step), short (a 2nd or 3rd) or long (an octave or so. Trombones use their slides, trumpets the half valve, and reeds a downward fingered gliss. The Snooky Young fall-off is lipped down by the trumpets and reeds. The trombones use fast slide movement. Fall-offs are non-measured and left to the discretion of the player(s).

fills: Melodic, chordal or rhythmic answers.

functional chord substitution: Replacing harmonies with other harmonies that conform to the tradition of tonic/dominant pull. The use of secondary chords (*ii, iii* and *vi*), secondary and applied dominants and chords borrowed from the minor modes (♭*III*, ♭*VI* and ♭*VII*), and some temporary modulations are also included.

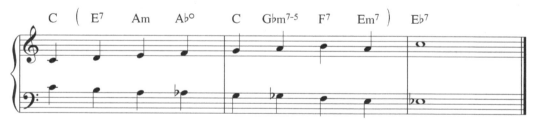

groove: The composite rhythm. Generally refers to combined repetitive rhythmic patterns in the rhythm section, but may also include the horns. Standard grooves may be notated by name (bossa nova, swing, ballad, etc.). Manufactured grooves will either combine elements of two or more grooves (i.e. drums play swing, while the bass plays a tango) or wholly new elements, which will need to be notated specifically.

head: Melody chorus.

hexatonic voicings: Generally a triad stacked on top of another triad. Two very useful varieties are a minor triad over another minor triad built a major 7th apart and augmented triads built a major 7th apart.

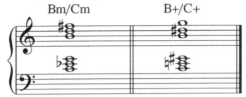

interlude: A contrasting form sandwiched between two chorus forms.

intro: Short for introduction.

inversion: Playing a motif upside down.

linearly derived harmonies: Harmonies that result from the confluence of melodic lines and don't conform to standard chord nomenclature.

mixed meter: regularly changing the meter signature or implying a superimposed meter.

modulation: Changing key. There are four basic types of modulation:

sequential: Repeating the last figure starting on a different pitch and continuing in the new key.

common tone: Holding over or repeating the last note from the old key to the new key.

dominant motion: Preceding the new key with its dominant.

modulation, continued:

abrupt (sudden): No preparation.

motif: Short melodic and/or rhythmic fragment.

non-functional (color) harmonic substitution: Replacing harmonies with chords outside the key without preparation. This can include parallel harmonies, triads over non-related bass notes, etc.

oblique motion: One voice repeats a pitch or pitches while another voice or voices move in parallel and/or contrary motion.

octave displacement: Changing the octave of one or several notes in a phrase.

octave unison: Two or more instruments playing the same pitch or pitches but separated by an octave.

pad: Harmonized chordal background consisting mainly of notes of longer duration. It used to be called "organ background."

parallel motion: Two or more voices moving in the same direction.

passing chords (sandwich chords): Interjecting smooth harmonies to create interest and avoid static harmonies. There are four basic methods:

diminished: Determine the anchor chords, voice them with the basic chord, and then build diminished chords on the in-between notes.

passing chords (sandwich chords), continued:

chromatic (planing): If the melody moves by half step or half steps, determine the anchor chords, voice them with the basic chord, and then working backwards, move the underparts chromatically in the same direction as the melody.

dominant: Determine the anchor chords, voice them with the basic chord, and then working backwards, build dominant 7th chords a perfect 5th above the upcoming chord. Very often altered dominants and tritone substitutes are used.

diatonic: When the melody moves stepwise in the key of the chord change, determine the anchor chords, voice them with the basic chord, and then working backwards, move all the voices stepwise in the key in the same direction as the melody. This is the least used of the four approaches, so although it is simple and non-chromatic, it can sound fresh.

peashooters: Brass instruments with small bores. They create a brighter sound than the normal size horn.

pedal point: Sustaining or repeating a pitch while the other voices move. Using the dominant is the most common, but tonic pedal point is also used. Most often the pedal is voiced below the other parts, but it can also be on top (often called inverted pedal point) or in the middle.

pixie mute: Originally called French straight mute or plug. A smaller version of the straight mute that fits in the bell of the horn beneath a plunger. A straight mute extends too far, and would prevent the plunger from covering the bell of the instrument.

plagal cadence: *IV I,* as in "Amen."

pyramid: Individual single note entrances that lay on top of the preceding entrances.

re-harmonization: Creating new harmonies to a previously existing melody. This can be a total re-vamping, isolated chords or something in between.

real sequence: Repeating a motif starting on a different pitch, and keeping all the intervals the same as the original. This results in stretching the tonality or leaving it altogether.

retrograde: Playing a motif backwards.

retrograde inversion: Playing a motif upside down and backwards.

ride pattern: The most common repetitive swing figure that drummers play on the ride cymbal. It can also be played on the crash cymbal or hi-hat.

riff: Motif that gets repeated. Very often the harmonies change beneath it.

Schenkerian analysis: A method of musical analysis of tonal music based on the theories of Heinrich Schenker (1868–1935). The goal is to extract the underlying structure of a tonal work and to show how the surface of the piece relates to this structure. (from Wikipedia)

syncopation: Accenting the weak beat or weak part of the beat, while avoiding the following strong beat or strong part of the beat.

scronch: Accented quarter note on beat 4. It can be short or tied over into the next measure. Either way it gets the chord that belongs to the next beat.

sectional writing: Scoring for groups of like instruments, i.e. trumpets, saxes, etc.

serialization: The ordering of notes. Serial music limits the pitches to a specific set of intervals. Other elements can also be serialized, like rhythm, dynamics and orchestration. The goal is to create concise, integrated pieces. 12-tone music uses a row of all 12 chromatic pitches and serializes the intervals. Rows can and often do contain fewer notes (3, 4, 5, etc.).

shout chorus (also known as the *sock chorus)*: The climax of the chart, where "everything comes together" and all the horns play.

slash chords: Generally triads over a related or non-related bass note. Sometimes triads or 7th chords over a different triad or 7th chord.

smear: Hitting a note flat and lipping up to the pitch. Alto saxophonist Johnny Hodges was legendary for this, but it is also used for expression on other horns and strings.

soli: A harmonized passage for two or more instruments playing the same rhythm.

song form: Generally 16, 32 or 12-bar forms (consisting of 4-bar or 8-bar phrases) that can be repeated and improvised on. The most common song forms in jazz nd the American Songbook are: *aaba, abac* (or *abab')* or *aab* (the Blues).

song form notation: Lower case italicized letters represent phrases, i.e. *abcd.* Repeated letters mean that the material repeats verbatim or verbatim with a different turnaround, i.e. *aaba.* Letters with an apostrophe represent phrases that start the same, and then go somewhere else, i.e. *abab'.* Generally standard song phrases are 8 bars in length, but on rare occasions, they could be 4 bars, 6 bars, 10 bars, 16 bars, etc. Here are some examples of well-known songs with these forms:

abcd *Stella By Starlight* (8-bar phrases)

aaba *Honeysuckle Rose* (8-bar phrases)

aab *The blues* (4-bar phrases)

abab' *There Will Never Be Another You* (8-bar phrases)

abac *Gone With The Wind* (8-bar phrases)

aaba+tag *Moonlight In Vermont* (6-bar *a* sections, 8-bar bridge, 4-bar tag)

spread chords or chorale voicings: Open voicings that generally have the root on the bottom.

stop time: A regular pattern of short breaks, often filled in by a soloist. The melody chorus of *Sister Sadie* or the Harlem Globetrotters' version of *Sweet Georgia Brown* are famous examples.

subtone: Way of playing reed instruments very softly, usually in the lower register. The effect is that we hear more air than tone.

swing: The perfect confluence of rhythmic tension and relaxation in music, creating a feeling of euphoria. Characterized by accented weak beats (democratization of the beat) and eighth notes that are played on the first and third eighth notes of an eighth note triplet. Duke Ellington defined swing as when the music feels like it is getting faster, but it isn't.

symmetrical voicings: Generally 6- or 8-note voicings that, if divided in half, will contain all different pitches but the same intervals. The intervals can be in the same vertical order or inverted.

tag or tag ending: Derived from vaudeville endings. The two most common are ||: IV/IV° I (second inversion) V/ii ii V :|| I and ||: iii V/ii ii V :|| I. Repeats are optional.

thickened line: Voicings that are constructed from the melody down, with everyone playing the same rhythm as the melody. These kinds of voicings generally omit the roots and are not concerned with inversions, since the bassist is stating the root progressions.

thumb line: A slow moving (half notes or slower) mostly stepwise unison or solo line used to accompany a melody. Thumb lines stay away from melody and bass notes, and mostly contain 3rds and 7ths.

tonal (or diatonic) sequence: Repeating a motif starting on another step of the scale, but not adding accidentals, so that you are still in the original key.

tritone interval: A diminished 5th or augmented 4th. This interval contains three whole steps.

tritone substitution: substituting a dominant 7th chord built a diminished 5th away from the original chord.

truncation: Shortening by lopping off the end of a motif, phrase, or passage.

turnaround: A series of chords that take us back smoothly to the first chord of a progression (usually the tonic). Although generally used to refer to the last two bars of an 8-bar phrase, *I vi ii V* and *iii vi ii V* are commonly called turnarounds wherever they occur.

tutti voicings: 4-part close ensemble voicings doubled throughout the brass and reeds. There are several variations, but the great majority fall into two categories: either the reeds double the trumpets in their register or an octave below. This is generally determined by the range of the lead trumpet. If he goes above the staff, the reeds are voiced an octave below.

unison: Two or more instruments playing the same pitch or pitches in the same octave.

upper structure triad: A non-related major or minor triad placed above a 7th chord.

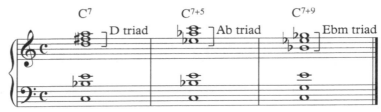

vamp: A repeated 2- or 4-bar chord progression usually supporting riffs. Coming from vaudeville, vamps are often used for intros, codas and interludes (especially just before a singer enters).

voicing: The specific pitches, inversion, and spacing that make up a chord.

Index

About the Author

Jazz composer, arranger, and conductor David Berger is recognized internationally as a leading authority on the music of

M.T. REGAN

Duke Ellington and the Swing Era. Conductor and arranger for the Jazz at Lincoln Center Orchestra from its inception in 1988 through 1994, Berger has transcribed more than 1000 full scores of classic recordings, including more than 500 works by Duke Ellington and Billy Strayhorn. Several of these transcriptions, and a number of original arrangements, were featured in the 2013 Broadway hit, *After Midnight.*

In 1996 Berger collaborated with choreographer Donald Byrd to create and tour *Harlem Nutcracker,* a full-length two-hour dance piece that expands the Tchaikovsky/Ellington/Strayhorn score into an American classic. The 15-piece band assembled to play this show has stayed together as the David Berger Jazz Orchestra, performing Berger's music in New York City and on tours throughout the United States and Europe.

Berger has written music for symphony orchestras, television, Broadway shows and films, and has composed and arranged for Duke Ellington, Jazz at Lincoln Center, Quincy Jones, and the WDR Big Band. He has also arranged for dozens of singers including Jon Hendricks, Betty Carter, Freda Payne, Natalie Cole, Rosemary Clooney, Madeleine Peyroux, Milt Grayson, Cécile McLorin

Salvant, Susan Graham, Denzal Sinclaire, Champian Fulton, Freddie Cole, Jessye Norman, and Kathleen Battle.

Berger has taught jazz arranging and composition for 30 years in the New York City area at the Juilliard School, Manhattan School of Music, The New School, William Paterson University, Montclair State University and Long Island University. In addition to private teaching, Berger travels around the U.S. doing clinics with high school and college jazz bands.

Residing in New York City, Berger is currently composing two musical comedy shows and served as the arranger and musical director for *Apollo Club Harlem;* which starred Maurice Hines, Dee Dee Bridgewater, Cécile McLorin Salvant, Kevin Mahogany and Margot Bingham.

www.SuchSweetThunderMusic.com
www.DavidBergerJazz.com

Other Books by David Berger

- *Life in D♭: A Jazz Journal*
- *Democracy In Action:*
  The High School Jazz Band Director's Handbook
- *Fancy Footwork: The Art of the Saxophone Soli*
- **COMING SOON:** With Chuck Israels:
  The Public Domain Song Anthology
- **COMING SOON:** *Creative Jazz Composing*
  and Arranging, Volume 2: Writing for Vocalists

Available from **www.SuchSweetThunderMusic.com**
and **Amazon.com**.

CDs by David Berger

- *Harlem Nutcracker* / David Berger & The Sultans of Swing
- *Doin' the Do* / David Berger & The Sultans of Swing
- *Marlowe* / David Berger & The Sultans of Swing
- *Hindustan* / David Berger & The Sultans of Swing
- *Champian* / Champian Fulton with
  David Berger & The Sultans Of Swing
- *I Had the Craziest Dream:*
  The Music of Harry Warren / David Berger Octet
- *Sing Me A Love Song: Harry Warren's*
  Undiscovered Standards / David Berger Jazz Orchestra
  with Freda Payne and Denzal Sinclaire
- *Old Is New* / David Berger Jazz Orchestra with
  Denzal Sinclaire

Available for download from **cdbaby.com, iTunes.com, allmusic. com, Amazon.com,** and **SuchSweetThunderMusic.com**.
You can find many jazz arrangements, compositions and transcriptions at **SuchSweetThunderMusic.com**.

Book Reviews

Life in D♭: A Jazz Journal

David Berger, renowned jazz composer, arranger, band leader and educator, tells you what it's like... from falling in love with jazz as a boy, to his first jobs as a musician and arranger... from international triumphs with the Jazz at Lincoln Center Orchestra, to heartbreak and success with his own Big Band. The chapter on transcribing alone is worth the price.

"David tells it like it is. A compelling read for every musician and music lover."

Quincy Jones
Producer/musician/composer/arranger

Fancy Footwork: The Art of the Saxophone Soli

"There's nothing better for unifying a sax section than studying and refining a well-crafted saxophone soli.... Extracted from David's extensive collection of compositions and arrangements, these solis cover a wide range of styles, tempos and levels of difficulty. I only wish I'd had this set years ago. My students would have been all over them!"

Stutz Wimmer
Jazz Band Director Emeritus, The Lovett School

Democracy In Action:
The High School Jazz Band Director's Handbook

The culmination of 40 years of teaching jazz, with proven techniques to help you bring a band to its highest potential. Techniques known only by top professionals—and the reasoning behind them—help you transform a band in as little as 15 minutes.

"I have been a high school jazz band director for 21 years, and this is the best book I've ever seen about teaching jazz band. If you want your band to sound authentic and swing hard, study this book from cover to cover. Guaranteed to make your band better!"

Josh T. Murray
Jazz Band Director, Rio Americano High School
Sacramento, CA

Made in United States
Troutdale, OR
03/14/2024